Modern
Enlightenment

PSYCHOLOGICAL, SPIRITUAL, AND
PRACTICAL IDEAS FOR A BETTER LIFE

AMY JOHNSON, PH.D.

ISBN: 1475123043

ISBN 13:   9781475123043

To Ora
I'm still amazed that guys like you really do exist.

Acknowledgments

It's virtually impossible to thank everyone I'd like to thank. But here's a start.

I'm so grateful to all the clients I've had over the years. You have not only allowed me to do what I love, but you have inspired me in ways you'll never know. Your openness, vulnerability, and willingness to change are remarkable. I admire each and every one of you for putting yourself out there and having the courage to face your shadows in the name of growth—*never* an easy path. And thank you for trusting me enough to try out my suggestions and ways of seeing things. Your hard work and experiences are the heart of this book.

Thank you to everyone who reads my newsletter each week and to anyone who has ever sent me a note of support, tweeted, shared, liked, or otherwise given me some nod of encouragement. Those little things quite literally gave me the steam it took to keep going. To my friends and coaching colleagues from all corners of the globe...can you believe how much fun this is? I am able to form real connections with you via Skype, email, and Facebook while sitting in my comfy home with my babies crawling around at my feet. They definitely never said "work" would look like this.

I have learned from so many wonderful mentors and teachers. I have taken what they taught me, built upon that knowledge and now teach others...just a few who have been especially influential and will recognize your influence on my work—Martha Beck, Michael Neill, Wayne Dyer, Byron Katie, Pema Chodron, and Marianne Williamson. *A Course in Miracle* and the *Tao Te Ching* have each had an enormous impact on my views.

Thank you to Sheila Oakes for your help editing this book. Your suggestions made *Modern Enlightenment* clearer and classier. Thank you for letting me still begin sentences with 'and' and 'but' and for letting me swear from time to time, but for knowing when to push back and challenge me to clean things up, too.

To my Mom—thank you for being a seeker yourself and for teaching me that I'm in charge of my own destiny. You bought me a copy of Zig Ziglar's *See You at the Top* when I was just a kid, had Wayne Dyer's books lying around the house for me to stumble upon before I was even out of middle school, and sent me to college with Marianne Williamson's *A Return to Love*. You are always my biggest cheerleader no matter what I'm doing and that has made all the difference in the world.

To Ora—you've been telling me I should write a book practically since our first date and you have gladly taken care of so many of the details of our life so that I could do it. You are the best husband and daddy ever and you make life so much better. Thank you for blowing my good-relationships-are-a-myth theory *way* out of the water.

And to my babies—Willow, I love seeing the person you are becoming. You are such a sweet, loving, and connected little girl. Your carefree spirit and innocence has inspired so much of this book, and you are the best motivation I can imagine for trying to be a little more Enlightened myself. Miller, you've been somersaulting inside of me as this book has come to life…I can't wait to see what you inspire and create in your time on this planet.

Permissions

My intention for this work is that it is widely shared with as many people as possible. Please feel free to reprint, publish, and share any part of this book with anyone who you think might benefit from it. If you do, please include the following with any portion you reprint:

Reprinted by permission of the author, Dr. Amy Johnson (www. DrAmyJohnson.com).

Contents

Contents

Contents

Introduction

I am proof that people can change.

Not that I was ever *terribly* unhappy—I wasn't. It's just that I was weighed down, unnecessarily. I was burdened by beliefs that didn't serve me and weren't true—beliefs like the world is unfair and struggle is to be expected.

I believed that everyday life wasn't supposed to be enjoyable, that's what vacations and holidays were for. Hard work was more laudable than taking the easy way and money was your reward for doing things you hated to do.

I heard that lazy and selfish were the two worst things you could be and I interpreted that to mean *doing* was much more important than *being*. And, that putting your own desires before someone else's was wrong, wrong, wrong.

I believed things could happen out in the world that were capable of destroying my happiness without my permission so I was always on guard against them. I was constantly scanning the horizon for what might go wrong, looking out for where I should brace myself, waiting for the other shoe to drop, and making sure to never get too happy or too comfortable because that's surely when tragedy would strike.

I spent most of the first twenty-five years of my life in survival mode, protecting myself from awful things that never happened and were never real to begin with. My only means of controlling the way I felt—I believed—was to give myself a nice buffer of accomplishments. If I could get the best grades, have the best boyfriend, be the right size, and choose the most exciting activities I'd be somewhat protected against whatever bad thing might happen. Happiness came from the outside. I didn't know there was another option.

I was overwhelmed by emotions I couldn't control. Shame for not being better. Anger at my parents for not being who I wanted them to be. Frustration with God and the Universe for not dropping me into more cushy circumstances. I had no idea that I had some say in how I handled my thoughts and emotions. I was a victim of whatever thought or mood struck.

Other people's reactions and moods determined mine. If a teacher smiled in approval, I was good enough; if not, I wasn't. If the people around me were having a bad day, I was too. I took on whatever labels and feelings people handed me, never knowing I had the right to refuse them; never knowing I had the power to decide how I felt.

I lived in reaction mode, simply reacting to what was thrown my way. I didn't know that creating my own experiences was an option. I didn't realize I could see things any way other than the automatic way they appeared to me.

In my teens and twenties I believed that truly happy relationships were a myth. I had never actually witnessed the kind of relationship I would have wanted. Besides, even if *some people* had good relationships, I knew I wouldn't be one of them. I had too many issues. I had too much baggage; too much inherited family history of bad relationships. As I got older, I was only attracted to older, married men. I figured my prospects of having a happy marriage and family were slim to none.

All of the beliefs, shame, and pressure eventually led to my developing a serious anxiety disorder in my early twenties. At its worst I was having upwards of thirty panic attacks a day and was virtually housebound. I was living alone, five hours away from my family and closest friends, and I was petrified to leave my apartment.

Like all challenges, this one was actually a gigantic blessing. It forced me to take a good look at my life—all of it, from the beliefs I held, to the way I treated myself and others, to the choices I was making. With a ton of professional help and lot of determination on my part, I did make it through my anxiety disorder. But my self-help took on a life of its own. An anxiety disorder was the last straw. I was fed up with the way my life was going and I was willing to do whatever it took to make it better.

That's when things started to change. Or, I should say, when I started to change them.

Life is much different today.

I no longer believe that life is hard. I still believe it's unfair, but it's been unfair in my favor many times so "unfair" seems like a pretty good thing. I now believe that doing nothing is one of the best choices you can ever make and that prioritizing your own desires is the kindest way to go.

I still love setting out to accomplish big things and dreaming up crazy adventures, but only because those things are fun in and of themselves. They're not a means to an end. I don't do them for someone else's approval. They don't guarantee anything and they don't provide lasting happiness; creating my happiness is my job independent of anything or anyone in my life.

I went from living almost completely reactively to living creatively much of the time. I can choose how I want to feel and create those feelings myself. I don't always do that, of course. I get sucked into other people's emotions and try to control circumstances at times, like we all do. But my emotions are so much more stable than they once were because they aren't determined by the people and things around me.

I still catch myself waiting for the other shoe to drop, wondering if it's really safe to be this happy. Instead of buying into that fearful story, I notice it, smile at the thought of how it used to be, and take my chances. The big bad terrible thing never happened before, so I bet it won't happen now. And even if it does, my worrying can't protect me from it or prevent it from happening in the first place.

I still hear that negative voice inside me whisper the internal story of how I'm not good enough. Who am I to think I could write a book, or help people run their lives, or be in a healthy relationship, or raise a couple kids? I hear it less than I used to, but it's still there and probably always will be.

When I do hear it, I immediately label it the "not-good-enough story" which takes most of the sting away and helps me to remember that these stories are more fiction than fact. It's just a recurring narrative my mind likes to replay. That doesn't mean I need to listen to it, or believe it, or act on it.

There was no flash of insight or single 'a-ha' moment that changed everything. It happened through a series of small changes to the way I viewed the Universe and my relationship to it. I made a series of new choices that were different from my old choices. This was all done with a heavy dose of awareness. I started looking at my life from the viewpoint of an objective observer who made no judgments and had no agenda. I learned to view things with curiosity rather than immediately evaluating them as good or bad, right or wrong.

Those small perspective changes and viewpoints are some of the things you'll read about in this book.

Is it good for you?

Life is good. Like, really good.

Fifteen years ago, I would've never believed it could be like this.

Bobby McFerrin singing "Don't Worry Be Happy" went right over my head. "Working for the Weekend" and "Hell is for Children" were playing from my personal boombox.

I looked right past all those yellow smiley face T-shirts epitomized in Forrest Gump and homed in on "Shit happens." All kinds of happy memories from my teenage years escape me, but I clearly remember a coffee mug in our house that said, "Life's a bitch and then you die."

Guess what? Life's not a bitch.

Now I see that's all just stuff that people tell themselves and choose to focus on, often for sake of fitting in with other humans. There's a strong biological drive to fit in. Unfortunately, it is strong enough to make us choose misery just because everyone else is miserable.

When you show up fully engaged in your life and stop buying into your own stories…

When you take total responsibility for your own happiness and wake up to the lies you've been telling…

Life gets *good*.

And it doesn't have to look perfect. I'm sarcastic, I swear, I get crabby, and things go wrong but I tell you, underneath it all, I'm happier than I ever thought possible.

So trust me, this life-is-good stuff is not just for the former cheerleaders and motivational speakers. You don't have to be super bubbly or gregarious or an extravert to find happiness. I'm none of those.

You *can* be happy underneath the rippling waves that life rolls across the surface. You don't do it by banishing struggle or sadness; you do it by recognizing what's always present underneath. It's coming to know that underneath the beliefs and the drama and the car breaking down and the baby getting sick, all is well.

Life is really good.

How to use this book

This book is part old, part new.

It's based on a collection of short pieces I've written over the past two years, many of which were published on my blog (www.DrAmyJohnson. com) and in my weekly newsletter. That's the "old" part.

There's also a lot of brand-new material written just for this book. There are new pieces that elaborate on previous material, revisions of my original blog posts that reflect new thinking, and additional pieces that serve to bridge some of the concepts together.

What I love about the structure of this book is that the Enlightenment comes in small doses. The pieces are short. They're organized by topic so you can read them in order, but they're also totally independent little nuggets of Enlightenment so you can skip around if you want.

You can read it cover to cover, or sneak in a few short pieces here and there. However you read it, try to do so with an open mind and an open heart. Try on, practice, and adopt the parts that resonate with you. This book is a collection of new perspectives. It presents different ways of seeing the things, people, and situations you encounter every day. Some of those new perspectives will feel good to you—they'll feel like they fit. Some won't.

In fact, you're going to read some things that go against most of what you've heard before. That's the point. This is a place to play with different perspectives and try them on. Do yourself a favor and consider some of the ideas before you dismiss them. Our minds put up enormous resistance to new beliefs. That's normal. The more your mind is fighting something, the more reason there is to take a look and see what that resistance is all about. It could be that it just doesn't fit with what your own intuition is telling you and that's fine. But it could also be that it's the exact thing you need to hear in that moment.

These perspectives have been tested out on my clients and they've brought them peace. I've tested them all on myself and if they didn't bring me peace, I didn't include them here. But remember, nothing works for everyone. If it doesn't jive with your intuition it's simply not for you. No harm done. Try something else on for size.

Life *is* good. Keep an open mind and see what you discover.

1

What Modern Enlightenment Is.
And What it Isn't.

This book is about experiencing more peace in your life. It's about living in a way that makes you the source of your own happiness rather than waiting for other people or circumstances to do that job for you.

It's also about those things you've always done—your deep-rooted habits and patterns—especially if you'd like to *stop* doing what you've always done. It's about checking in with what you're thinking and feeling from time to time and beginning to *choose* how you think and feel rather than be a victim of your thoughts and emotions.

It's about loving and accepting yourself. It's about *really* loving and accepting yourself. And loving and accepting other people, too. It's also about having easy relationships that don't resemble a roller-coaster in any way (Except that they're fun. And exciting. And worth the wait.)

Oh, and it's also about asking for guidance and tapping into a crazy universal energy that's much bigger than all of us.

There's a lot covered in this book and it all comes down to one basic idea: becoming just a little more Enlightened today than you were yesterday.

Modern Enlightenment

Enlightenment is achievable by anyone—including you.

Enlightenment is gained by simple shifts and small steps; by developing new perspectives and better ways of being. Enlightenment is achieved by making small tweaks to how you see and interact with the world. It comes from being just a little more awake and aware in your own life. This isn't your Grandma's Enlightenment. It's not Enlightenment done the way some old-school sage or guru would have you do it.

It's not achieved by taking a vow of silence, or spending hours in meditation, or always turning the other cheek. You don't have to give away all your stuff, or stop swearing, or quit your corporate job to be Enlightened.

This is Enlightenment the modern way. It's practical and down-to-earth. It's Enlightenment for navigating this particular time on the planet because you *can* live in the modern world with compassion, kindness, and self-acceptance. In fact, I highly recommend it.

Modern Enlightenment is about letting go, and realizing you don't have to try to control things anymore. Things work out pretty well—better, actually—when you take a step back and let them unfold. No need to force them to look like what your limited perspective thinks they should look like.

Modern Enlightenment is about radical acceptance of What Is. This means accepting your circumstances, people in your life, and yourself. It means not wasting your time wishing things were different, but accepting exactly What Is *and then* creating what you want when and where you can.

Modern Enlightenment is about being fluid. Not rigid. Its about being easy and willing to change. Holding tightly to beliefs and latching on to thoughts is the opposite of Modern Enlightenment. Modern Enlightenment is approaching those ideas that run through your mind with curiosity, not with attachment.

Modern Enlightenment is about taking total responsibility for the state of your life. Responsibility is the opposite of blame, by the way. I'm not talking about blaming yourself for what's there, I'm talking about accepting whatever it is and choosing where you want to go from there. Your happiness is *your* business, no one else's.

Modern Enlightenment is about doing things that scare you. You don't wait around until the conditions are right before you act, but decide what you want to do and do it, fear and all.

Modern Enlightenment is about paving your own path. It's about leading your own life. It's not about following the rules, using someone else's blueprint, or relying too much on what the experts say. Your life is yours to design and create. You're the architect here.

2

Whose Underwear
Are You Wearing?

Isn't it cool that there are people who are really passionate about algebra? And chemistry and dry cleaning and accounting? Thank God for those people, because I love a good dry cleaner and it would suck to have to do that myself.

Think about all the people who are stuck doing stuff they don't love. They're trying to jam themselves into a mold that doesn't quite fit—it's like living a life that's not really yours, and going through the motions of something that doesn't feel quite right.

Maybe you know firsthand what it feels like to live a life that doesn't seem to really belong to you.

I don't believe that our passions are random.

I believe that if something gets you excited, there's a reason for it. I don't care if it's algebra or watching *General Hospital*. If it seriously feels good—and I don't mean the "I'd rather watch *General Hospital* than organize my closets" good, but the you-have-a-real-physical-inspiration-and-genuine-excitement-about-it kind of good—then that's what you're meant to be doing.

If you have that kind of passion about becoming an artist, or starting a business, or adopting a puppy but your mind keeps telling you, "you're not good enough," "there's no money in that," "there's poop involved," respectfully tell your mind that you appreciate it's opinion but please stay out of this. And then follow the inspiration because I guarantee, it's not for nothing.

What if everyone just did exactly what they most loved to do in life? Wouldn't it be cool if the number of people who would truly love to be vacuum cleaner sales reps or cardiac surgeons were perfectly equal to the number of vacuum cleaner sales reps and cardiac surgeons the world needs?

Maybe if everyone followed what they were most passionate about, we'd all fit perfectly into our place in the world like a puzzle coming together. We'd all be authentically ourselves doing what we love everyday. Think about how good we'd all be at what we did and how smoothly the world would run. You'd never think, "Am I qualified?" or "Is there a market for that?" Your passion would qualify you.

Instead, it's like we're all trying to fit ourselves into clothes that don't fit. Not everyone—some people are doing what they're meant to be doing. But far too many of us are wearing someone else's underwear. And they are cutting off our circulation.

Find a nice pair that fits. And do whatever it takes to wear them everyday.

3

If Nothing Ever Changed, Could You Be as Happy as You Want to Be?

The power was out on much of the East Coast last weekend. Some people were *really* affected by the outage. You've seen them—they are the ones who get interviewed by the local news or *The Weather Channel*. Their lives are put on hold until power is restored. They have no control over when their power will come back because they rely entirely on external power sources.

At the other extreme are people who weren't impacted by the outage at all, usually because they have their own generators. They don't rely on getting their power from external sources so when the external sources break down they carry on as if nothing has happened.

Who are you more like? Where do you get your power? By the way, I'm not talking about electricity anymore. *I'm talking about personal power.* Do you pull yours from external sources or generate your own?

Your Power Source

There comes a time in almost everyone's life when you realize you don't need anything to be happy. You know that if nothing ever changed—if this was it—you could be just as happy as you want to be.

Maybe that realization comes in a series of fleeting moments. Or maybe it hits you all at once and changes everything. For many people, it comes when they're defeated by the outside world (their externally supplied power goes out) and they give up expecting things to be different. They surrender to What Is.

When you surrender, you realize there's something operating under the surface. Something *inside of you* that generates peace. It turns the old, external power model on its head. The old external power model goes like this: if you want to feel better than you feel right now you should think about the external changes that would make you feel better. Then you should run out and make those things happen.

The new, generator model says external stuff makes you feel better for a while, but it's not sustainable. And it's certainly not reliable. In the new model, you get to feel how you want to feel *now*. You don't have to wait for outside conditions to catch up because you have an internal happiness generator.

It's okay to work by the old model. Achieving goals is fun, getting stuff is fun, bettering your life circumstances will certainly add joy…to an extent.

It's just that instead of working *only* by the old model, you can work the new model, too. Working both angles puts you in the sweet spot because you get to chase external goals without *needing* to achieve them. You get to go for the promotion or lose the weight just for the sake of being promoted and feeling better. Not because your happiness depends on it. It takes all the pressure off.

The goals are mostly irrelevant to your happiness. They're like nabbing the prime parking spot at grocery store. It's nice, but not necessary. You can still get all the groceries on your list no matter where you park.

When you're not dependent on the goals, you're not attached to them. Then, if for whatever reason, the promotion doesn't come through or the weight doesn't come off, you don't have to be so distraught. The only thing that will have happened is that you didn't get your promotion or you don't fit into your skinny jeans.

It's not like you have to be unhappy because of it.

Part I

Understanding and
Breaking Old Patterns

"I just looked at the pattern of my life, decided I didn't like it, and changed."

—David Sedaris

Patterns are our automatic, default ways of being. You see it in the way you snap at your husband/mistress/kids/cat when you are under stress. Or, how you find yourself in the same bad relationship over and over again.

Or, the way you use shopping or cupcakes or pot to avoid feeling what life throws at you.

Patterns are old and deep. They're often based on a belief or set of beliefs we formed in a split second a long time ago.

Examining our patterns is our chance to re-examine what we once decided, and to see if those thoughts and beliefs still work in our current life. It's our chance to choose what we want today instead of living out an old choice that may not apply anymore.

Patterns may be what we do, and they reveal what we think, but they're not us. We're much more than a collection of conditioned responses.

It can be tricky to figure this out because these patterns feel like us. People tell me all the time, "That's just what I do," "It's who I am," "I've always been this way."

And I say, "What's your point?"

Just because you formed a belief one day long ago…and a corresponding set of emotions and behaviors formed around that belief…and that whole mash up of stuff turned into a habit…it does not mean you are destined to be a slave to it forever. Not even close. You can change your patterns as soon as you are ready to put in the effort required to change.

To start, all you need is a tiny bit of motivation and about an ounce and a half of awareness.

Become aware of what triggers your pattern and the impact the pattern has on your life.

Become an authority on that thing you do and those subjective viewpoints you espouse.

Look at yourself in the mirror. Notice how others see you.

Then decide—as in choose—if that's really what you want to be doing.

Is it?

Is this the way you want to operate? Is this the impact you want to have on the world? Is this the legacy you want to leave, the impression you want to make, or the way you want to feel?

If so, that's awesome—don't change a thing. If not, it's time to make a change. This section will show you how.

4

What's the Big Ass Disaster (BAD) that Shaped the Rest of Your Life?

Humans assign meaning to everything.

That's what we do. Our brains are wired for it.

When something good happens and especially when something bad happens we go to work figuring it out and making it mean something. It plays out something like this: A Big Ass Disaster (BAD) occurs when you are a kid. It's often the first really negative or scary thing you remember. Maybe your dad moves out, a sibling is born and everything changes, or your parents accidentally leave you at the grocery store.

For my client Rick, it was when he watched his mom have a stroke as she was ironing shirts and he and his brother were watching cartoons. He was five; his little brother was two. Your disaster doesn't necessarily have to be that big or that bad, by the way.

In the moment the disaster strikes, your little kid brain makes it mean something. Specifically, you decide the event means something about you and how you have to be from then on.

Rick remembers realizing life was never going to be the same. As his mom lay on the floor, the hot iron sizzling through the shirts, and his little brother crying and yelling for mommy to wake up, Rick decided he'd have to be in charge from now on.

At five years old, he also instantly realized he didn't know how to be charge. So the meaning he created went something like this: I have to take care of everything and I don't know how.

A five-year-old mind drew those conclusions, and an adult man has lived by them every day since.

Thirty-six years later, Rick still holds onto beliefs like, "I'm in charge," and "Everything's on my shoulders," and "I'm the only one who can do it." As if that's not bad enough, what makes those beliefs especially troublesome is that he also holds onto beliefs like, "I can't handle it," "I'm not sure what to do," and "Am I really cut out for this?"

By most anyone's standards, Rick is an extremely successful man. He's a leader in his business and community. With beliefs like, "I'm in charge now," his success is not difficult to predict.

But he also has the constant nagging feeling that he's not ready for the challenges he takes on. He's not good enough. He doesn't know how. Those beliefs keep him swirling in a self-defeating cycle of doubt and fear. His typical pattern is that he steps up to the challenge and then freaks out in anxiety and uncertainty about his abilities.

The conclusions that made sense to a scared little five-year-old completely drive his emotions and behaviors today.

Where are You a Slave to Beliefs You Made Up as Child?

To find out, think about your own BADs—we usually have a few, although one might stand out above all others. If you are having a hard time finding yours, remember it's probably centered on one of the earliest vivid, negative memories you have. Most likely, but not always, you were between the ages of two to six years old. If you are coming up blank those are ages to start.

Find one? Good. Now really re-create the scene in your mind. Try to see the all the details around you, smell the smells, hear the sounds, and most of all, feel the feelings you felt. Be there a little longer. I realize it's not a fun place to hang out. The good news is that if it upsets you to think about the incident, you've probably tapped into the big one for you.

In the moment the disaster struck, what were you feeling?

What were you thinking?

What did you tell yourself about fixing the disaster or preventing another one? Your little kid mind formulated a plan. Rick's plan was to be in charge. What was yours?

How did you feel about carrying out your plan? What did it mean about you as a person?

How would your life change to support that plan?

Now you are getting somewhere.

How does that little kid's plan play out in your life today? What is the pattern? That's how you are a slave to beliefs you made up as a child. And that's where you will start when it comes to unraveling the pattern so that you can live by your own free will.

5

My BAD. Or How I Decided to Be Quiet

To help you to discover your own BADs, here's one of mine.

My mom was dating a man I strongly disliked. I thought I'd be really mature about the situation and have a talk with her about finally dumping him, once and for all. I was about nine years old.

In my mind, this conversation was definitely going to change things. I mean, who can resist the thought-out, logical appeal of a nine-year-old? My arguments were foolproof. I was sure my reasoning was very sound.

I made my case. And was promptly informed that she will date who she wants, thank you very much, and I'd be smart to get used to it.

In that moment—I can remember exactly where I was sitting (at the head of my purple bed, knees drawn to my chest) and the look on her face (matter-of-fact, a little sympathetic but not about to compromise). I said to myself: "My opinion doesn't matter here so I might as well keep it to myself. I'm not putting myself out there like that anymore."

And so began a pattern. From that day forward, I hesitated to give my opinion. I only shared myself when it was clear that my opinion was wanted (and since I was the one defining "clear," it never was). I waited until someone directly asked me how I felt before offering up anything.

You may have noticed that when you don't openly share yourself or offer up your opinions, you eventually teach people to stop asking. No one wants to constantly pull information out of you, no matter how much they love you. It's up to each of us to offer our opinion, not to wait to be asked for it.

Just like Rick, the beliefs I invented as a child were carried into adulthood. They showed up everywhere because that's how patterns work. How you do anything is how you do everything. My beliefs became generalized and I mindlessly applied them all over the place.

I've been aware of this particular BAD for awhile. I can clearly see the beliefs I formed and how those beliefs have impacted my life.

Being aware doesn't mean those beliefs no longer affect me. Awareness is the first necessary step, but it's not necessarily the end of the pattern.

But from a place of awareness I can be on the look out for when I'm quietly trying to fade into the wallpaper, biting my tongue because no one has asked for my opinion.

And I can consciously override that pattern—over and over until it gets easier. That's what I've been doing for the past few years, and it's been working.

I have been consciously overriding the pattern and questioning the beliefs I formed, too. I start breaking the pattern with questions like: Is it really true that people don't want my opinion? Can I know that just because they haven't asked, they don't care? Does it even matter whether they want my opinion or not?

Challenging your patterns, when made a daily practice, is how you begin to transform them. That's how awareness of your BAD lets you turn BAD into good.

6

How Old Do You Feel?

This is one of my favorite questions—especially when someone is feeling scared or overwhelmed.

How old do you feel right now?

When you are looking at a pile of stuff to put away and a mess in your office and a million things to start and you can't bring yourself to do just one thing, how old do you feel?

Let's say you feel eight. Let yourself go back there. What was life like at eight? When did you feel overwhelmed at eight? When did you feel lost and couldn't do just one thing?

If you ask yourself, "How old do I feel right now?" and you get an answer or flashback right away, there's a good chance your overwhelm today is you reliving something from the past.

It has nothing to do with today. Your inner eight-year-old is calling the shots.

And it's funny, isn't it....you wouldn't trust an eight-year-old to make your decisions as an adult, would you?

But are you?

This is where people usually look at me in a defeated, helpless way. "The pattern has been running since I was eight, I guess I'm stuck with it."

Um, no. Just become aware of it and then act differently. Here's how it works:

If you feel overwhelmed today:

- Ask yourself how old you feel—maybe you remember how you tried to take care of your drunken mom when you were eight and felt snowed under all the time.
- See that your issue today is not at all related to an eight-year-old caring for a drunken mom. It's triggering that, but it's not that.
- Act differently. Even when it's uncomfortable and you are not sure what to do, do something different anyway.

It's not going to feel comfortable but luckily, comfort is not a prerequisite for change. In fact, discomfort is a good sign that you are on the right track.

7

How You Do Anything is How You Do Everything

I've been drawn to this expression for a while, not really understanding it intellectually but totally getting it on some intuitive level. It felt right-on, although I didn't understand what it meant.

Does it do anything for you?

It's all about patterns. For example, how do you react when you are confronted? Do you get instantly defensive? Do you counter-attack, showing them they messed with the wrong person? Or do you assume they're right and try to figure out what you did wrong?

How do you approach learning something difficult? When you make a mistake, do you get frustrated? Laugh at yourself? Blame the teacher? Cry?

Author Geneen Roth talks about how patterns work with food. Our relationship with food is a mirror for our relationship with life. Do you deprive yourself of food (life) and then binge on it when no one is looking? Do you stand in front of the refrigerator forever, unable to make a decision? Or do you grab something without thinking and later wish you had thought it through more?

How you approach food is how you approach life.

It's true with money, too. Do you hoard money, afraid to let it go? Do you spend as if there's no tomorrow? Do you worry about it, constantly count it, or ignore it?

How you approach money is how you approach life. Apparently, how you approach anything is how you approach life.

One of my patterns is this: I look for the "right" formula and believe that if I don't do it exactly right, I'm not deserving of the full benefit. If I do all the crunches "right" but skimp a little on the last one, I might as well have not done them at all. I mean, why would I get any benefit since I didn't do it All The Way? What good are 14 ½ crunches? The instructor did 15, so she wins, I lose.

I loved psychology so I got a PhD in it. Why do it half-assed? We unpacked one third of the boxes on the first day of moving into our new home so I might as well do them all. Who needs sleep?

It's not hard to see how the way I do crunches is the way I do life.

Here are some patterns my clients have uncovered:

The girl who always has to be noticed. She speaks up in every group and has to have the last say in the Monday morning meeting. She can't understand why her boyfriend has become really quiet and withdrawn throughout their relationship. Come to think of it, every boyfriend has done that. She thinks her pattern is that she picks guys who are talkative at first and then become withdrawn. Her real pattern is that she can't handle not being the center of attention.

The guy who thinks no one treats him well enough. He thinks this about his wife, his kids, his parents, and the teenager who took his order at Subway. He gets no respect, everywhere. He cut his parents out of his life years ago. Now he's cutting his kids out of his life, but it's only because they treat him so poorly.

The lady who really loves shoes. She simply loves them and it seems innocent enough, but…… She just has to run out and shoe shop when she has a bad day at work or when her daughter talks back to her or when she feels fat. It's the weirdest thing—in the middle of a fight with her husband the other day, she felt the need to go online and look at shoes. Isn't that strange?

Do any of these ring a bell with you? What are some of your patterns?

8

What I Learned from the Horses

One thing about patterns is that they're *pervasive*. Your patterns show up in all parts of your life. The way you do anything is the way you do everything.

I learned how pervasive our patterns are from horses.

I once had the opportunity to do some horse whispering. The objective is to get in the pen and invite the horse to join up with you. You basically invite him to follow you around in circles.

How do you invite the horse? They told me that the horse would respond to my energy. I was told to see the horse doing what I wanted him to do. The idea was to use my energy to invite him to play follow the leader.

Because horses read and respond to nonverbal energy, if you are deemed trustworthy, safe, and command authority, the horse joins. If not, you are standing in the middle of the pen with a horse who won't give you the time of day. Or worse, a horse who is scared or acts aggressively toward you.

Here's where patterns come in. The strong woman with the Brooklyn accent who didn't take any crap—the one we all knew to have bold, almost aggressive energy—scared her horse to death. The horse bucked, kicked, and was in full self-protection mode the instant she walked into the pen.

When the small, quiet woman who described herself as a "chronic doormat" walked into the pen, her horse didn't even notice her. She stood there trying to summon the right energy to make her horse follow, but the horse was blind to her.

The woman everyone confided in, the natural leader who could just as easily lead a business meeting as take a back seat and contribute humbly, the one who exuded confidence but was nothing but kind and always seemed to know what she wanted...*her* horse was interested.

When she walked into the pen, her horse noticed. He didn't try to attack her and he didn't hide from her. He walked right up to her with his own confidence.

He bowed his head to her, the horse sign of deference and respect. He brushed his head against her shoulder, the horse sign for "let's be friends."

When she began walking in circles, he followed. When she stopped, he stopped. When she ran, he ran.

This is how she is in life. How all the women were in the pen is how they are in life. It's their pattern, their pervasive and automatic way of being in the world.

Horses see it and you see it in others, if not in yourself. You see how people show up the same way in all aspects of their lives.

Can you see it in yourself? Take a look at how others respond to you and your energy. Do they join up easily? Do they brush their head against your shoulder?

How do you experience others? Are they closed off? Drama-filled? Too close or too distant?

That's not really them. It's them reflecting you back to you.

It's them being your mirror.

9

How Do You Win?

Every family has a way of keeping score. Often unspoken—but sometimes blatantly official—there are rules for what's good and bad; right and wrong. I call it The Family Game.

Each family makes up the rules for how to win at their Game. The rules are passed down from generation to generation. Some generations—and some individuals—buy into The Game more than others. But to some extent, the rules are encoded in each and every member of the family. To identify your Family Game, ask yourself, "How do I win in this family?" Which behaviors or traits most lead to approval and admiration?

Families might have more than one Game, but there are usually one or two primary Games. Many families play the same Game because The Game is influenced by society.

I spent the Labor Day weekend with my husband's family. In his family, The Game is Who-Works-Hardest? In his family, working hard is physical labor in the external world, doing things like building and fixing; cleaning and cooking. In his family, the one Who-Works-Hardest wins.

Actually, the Who-Works-Hardest Game is one of the most common I've seen. I think most families have some version of this Game, although it takes on different flavors based on how they define hard work. In other families, Who-Works-Hardest looks like Who-Has-The-Best-Career? Or Who-Is-Busiest? Or Who-Has-The-Most-Kids? So even in the Who-Works-Hardest Game, each family has their own unique spin that determines the specific rules.

I have a client whose Family Game is Who-Sacrifices-Most? If you give up your own needs for your kids, your neighbors, or your church, you win.

A friend's Family Game is Who-Endures-The-Most-Physical-Pain? They're constantly competing to see whose ailments are most painful, who was in labor longest, who has had the most surgeries, or who has the most allergies. The sickest one wins.

What's your Family's Game? Can you see how it impacts your life? You probably can't see all the ways because there are so many. Do you always follow the rules? If so, you might not even recognize it as The Game. One rule in my Family's Who-Works-Hardest Game is "don't do anything that could be considered lazy." Lazy buys you an automatic disqualification. When my Grandpa was in the hospital, sick and near death, he repeatedly announced that he needed to just relax and be lazy. As if he was asking permission despite his illness, to be out of The Game. That's how strong The Game is.

Do you recognize The Game, but think it doesn't affect your behavior? Trust me, it does. Maybe you try really hard to not play the Family Game, but I guarantee part of you feels guilty or uncomfortable or like an outcast when you are not following the rules.

Maybe your life is set up to rebuke the rules of The Game. You'll show them what you think of their damn game. Except rebelling against the rules goes against your programming which means it takes a lot of energy. So, by fighting The Game you are actually more sucked into it than you think.

Do you think of the Family Game as being simply "who you are"? Of course it is. And there's nothing wrong with that, unless it would feel like freedom to drop The Game. You drop The Game by making up your own rules, rules that you consciously choose, that work in your life today.

It's your choice. How do you want to win?

10

How I Sabotage My Marriage

Humans love stability and balance.

So much so that even good changes can feel uncomfortable. Winning the lottery, having your life story turned into a movie, publishing your book...these are all awesome, but panic-inducing, too.

Just like thermostats, we have a set point. Diverging too far from our internal average leaves us feeling vulnerable. Feeling vulnerable is no fun at all.

In his book *The Big Leap*, Gay Hendrix calls this the Upper Limit Problem. Basically, we all have our own upper limit for how much success, happiness, closeness, or abundance we're able to feel without totally freaking out. Exceeding our own set point can feel so uncomfortable that we're prone to self-sabotage. If we excel too much, we'll shoot ourselves right back down to what we're used to. We don't do it consciously; we do it through our comfort-seeking automatic patterns.

What this might look like in relationships is complaining about something minor or picking a fight when things are going really well. What this might look like in business is making a risky decision just as the business starts turning a profit. Or getting sick and not being able to speak at that big event. Or deciding to change your fulfillment center just as a slew of new orders comes in. What this might look like in terms of your health is bingeing as soon as you hit your goal weight or pulling a muscle a week before a race.

My Upper Limit Issue

I've been feeling a little anxious lately about how well things are going. Thinking about how blessed I am has been triggering thoughts of how awful it would be to lose it all.

It can be scary when you have a lot because you have a lot to lose.

Here's a thought I've had: My marriage and family life are almost too good to be true. The other night, I was thinking about how much I love having my husband around and how awful it would be if he weren't here. My healthy appreciation turned into my feeling somewhat needy. I love him in a detached, unconditional, nothing-to-with-me way, but this time I was feeling kind of clingy about it, in an I-might-not-be-okay-without-him kind of way.

A few hours later, I got really mad at him for something that wasn't his fault. It happened FAST. There was no conscious input, logic, or reasoning on my part. It happened almost as if I was on automatic pilot.

The next morning as I wondered how I turned so quickly from full appreciation to anger, I remembered the Upper Limit Problem. Maybe my family life was pushing up against my upper limits for how much good I can handle.

Maybe it was the fear of needing him that felt scary, so I got mad at him because that little bit of distance felt safer. Feeling too close was too vulnerable. Maybe my old story, "I don't need anyone—I can take care of myself—and good thing, because you can never really count on anyone, anyway," felt familiar and comfortable.

If it was about feeling too good, it's a classic Upper Limit Problem. If it was due to feeling too needy, it's still about letting a destructive pattern run in order to avoid feeling something I think I can't handle.

Either way, my instant anger wasn't at all about the thing I claimed to be angry about. When it happens fast and without your input, it's a fair bet that whatever is igniting your anger is NOT about what you are saying it's about.

That's a perfect time to get conscious and aware. It's time to choose your reactions instead of letting your patterns run you.

I thought of other times I face my Upper Limit Problem. When else do I knock myself down a few rungs to feel safer?

When I notice my self-sabotage, it's time to get über aware and not let the automatic patterns call the shots. It's time to get conscious and deliberate and make choices based on what I know I really want, not what my Upper Limits dictate.

Where are your upper limits? Is the discomfort of change keeping you small?

11

The Truth About Drama

Do you attract drama?

If you have a lot of drama-filled people or situations in your life, I'm about to say something you won't like.

It might be time to look in the mirror.

Yes, they may be crazy. I totally give you that. It may honestly, without a doubt, be all their stuff that's coming up and causing trouble. But if it keeps showing up in your life—even when you are not the cause of it—it's time to look at yourself.

It's time to take a peek. Not with blame or judgment. Self-reflection is never about blame or judgment. Instead, it's about looking with objectivity and interest.

Why might you be attracting this drama? Are you attracting it, or is it really a coincidence? Could there be something about you that triggers it? Do you ask for it or invite it in some unconscious, unintentional way?

Do you tell stories about your drama? Does it benefit you in some way? Even if the punishment is greater than the reward, *is* there a reward? Maybe it takes the focus off of you, or gives you something to do?

We teach people how to treat us. How are you teaching people to treat you? Deepak Chopra says one marker of wholeness is no longer having negative or drama-filled people and circumstances in your life. When you get in touch with your core and you feel connected to everything in life, drama falls away. I believe this because I've seen it a million times. Some people always have drama. Some people never do.

It's not a contest, but the level of drama in your life—even when it's totally other people's stuff—says something about you. About where you are, how you think, and the way you view your connection to other people and the universe.

How much drama floats around you? How will you choose to own it?

12

Projection and Parenting

Projection is fascinating, isn't it?

You are projecting when you attribute your feelings or thoughts to someone else. You assume they think and feel the way you do. Or, you see and treat them in a way that's completely colored by your own stuff.

It's very easy to project. It is especially easy to project onto a non-verbal being who you'd really love to understand. This could be why my husband and I used to project all over our poor dogs. I used to say, "Look how mad Buddha is that I have to go on this damn work trip. She really hates my boss and she can't wait until I can quit this job; it's written all over her furry little face."

Then we had a baby. We take her to a music class every week. She's one of about ten kids and is the youngest by far. She is the only crawler and the only one who isn't talking yet, or doing much of the formal dancing, singing, or instrument playing. Hubby and I let our personal stuff ooze all over pre-verbal Willow. Poor little blank slate gets all varieties of our projected crap.

Most of the music class is spent sitting in or dancing around a circle. When Willow crawls or wiggles out of formation, and is more interested in being in the middle of the circle, or when she's chewing on another kid's pants, or trying to nurse from the chest of the woman next to us, I cheer her on. You go, girl! Circle, schmircle—don't conform to what everyone else is doing! Make a mess! Break the rules! Rebel!

Truth be told, I have problems with authority. I'm afraid to conform. I'm afraid of being controlled, following the crowd, being boxed in, being average or even worse, being boring. I always have been. It's all my stuff.

Hubby couldn't be less like me in that respect. He likes structure (which is what he calls the thing I call conformity). He loves to fit in, and thinks things work better when everyone knows his or her role. He has no fear of being boxed in—his fear is of being an outcast, making waves, or being disruptive. So while Willow is unbuttoning the shirt of the mama next to us, his anxiety is through the roof. He's trying to rein her in. I'm laughing and encouraging her to express herself.

You can imagine our conversation on the car ride home. When it comes to parenting Willow, it's a constant game of push and pull. I'm pushing her out front, and giving positive reinforcement when she does something anti-norm; and he's pulling her in, teaching her that good little girls don't make a scene.

Push, pull; push, pull. (Just so you know, we aren't literally pushing or pulling our baby, or even openly disagreeing between us. What it actually ends up looking like is a pretty healthy compromise where she wanders just outside our reach for most of the class. It only feels like anxiety-driven pushing and pulling to us.)

I have my ideas about the traits I want to encourage in her and he has his. Neither is right or wrong. Or, more accurately, neither is more right or more wrong. And it's HARD for me to say that because I deeply feel that my way is better. But I know that it's not—that's just my stuff talking.

It's all our stuff—our patterns. It's so interesting to watch how we do that; how we see the world through our highly personalized lenses. We have such wildly different perceptions, yet as soon as we recognize and name the patterns and realize what we're doing to our cute little innocent blank slate, it tends to drop away.

Once the patterns are out in the open, the sting lessens. I can relax a little when she's being "too good" and he can relax a little when she's being "too bad."

See it for yourself in your own life. Where are you projecting? Can you notice it and let yourself relax a little, let go of your stuff, and turn off the projector?

13

What to Do with Your Patterns

You've uncovered some of your patterns. Now what?

Patterns are like zoo animals. They don't respond well to taunting. And they didn't do anything wrong, so there's no reason to taunt them, anyway. Please don't use them to beat yourself up and don't get mad at them or blame them for anything in your life.

Instead, simply observe them. Be interested, not judgmental. Become a scientist or a detective, noticing and observing and dissecting your patterns with complete objectivity. Or as close to complete objectivity as you can get. It sounds crazy, but try to appreciate them. Think of them as interesting information. Love them. They are going to help you grow.

Our patterns aren't stable or fixed. They can be picked apart and rearranged. You can play with them but first you've got to catch them in the act. When you notice a pattern you fall into, try to step in with awareness and purposely do things differently, just to see what happens.

For example, if you are that guy who feels like no one treats him with respect, next time you notice yourself feeling disrespected stop and pretend that the person you are talking to respects you. Even if you don't believe it, try it on and see how it feels to see things the way you want them to be. If you are the woman who has to buy shoes when she feels agitated, notice the urge to shop and do the opposite. Sit still and don't buy shoes. Then observe what happens.

Warning: this is going to be uncomfortable. Patterns are habits, but they often exist to distract you from some kind of pain. The discomfort that arises when we don't automatically fall into our patterns is what you can learn from. Sit with it until it begins to dissipate. It won't take as long as you think.

Beware of the tendency to dig too deeply into figuring out where your patterns come from or why they're there. Although knowing where they come from can shed some light, knowing their origins is not necessary for changing them. It's like the connect-the-dots puzzle. It doesn't matter which dot you start with, the game is in connecting them all and discovering the picture they create.

Rather than ask where it came from or whose fault it is, ask yourself some different questions. You might try:

- How does this pattern serve me today? What feelings, thoughts, or memories does it allow me to avoid?
- How does this pattern hold me back today?
- When is this pattern most likely to show up?
- What would I rather do in those situations?
- What might be possible if I gave up this pattern?
- What's one way I can begin to play with this pattern?
- Am I truly willing to be uncomfortable for a little while in order to change this pattern?

Questions like these will get you on the right track.

14

Replacing Old Patterns:
What Would You Do?

"When patterns are broken, new worlds emerge."
—Tuli Kupferberg

You may have heard that "nature abhors a vacuum." I'm no physicist, but I think it basically means that unfilled spaces go against the laws of nature. When there is a big empty space, something's going to rush in to fill it. This also works with changing patterns. When you get rid of an old habit, a new one will rush in to take its place.

You've heard of the people who have gastric bypass surgery and become addicted to alcohol or drugs. When their reliance on overeating to calm themselves is taken away, a new vice creeps right in to do the job. Or when people stop smoking and they gain weight. What's often happening is the ex-smoker has swapped one self-soothing habit for another.

So when you are trying to stop doing something, it's a good idea to think about what you might want to do instead. When you are trying to change something about yourself, think about how you'd *like to be*, and focus on the new behavior instead of focusing on what you currently do.

When you have a clear idea of how you'd like to be you can take action you consciously choose. When your automatic pattern starts running, you have a back-up plan and a clear alternative to flip to. You'll be in a place from which to make a better choice.

It's like those bracelets that used to be everywhere that asked What Would Jesus Do (WWJD?) Ask yourself—if you weren't a slave to your patterns—what would *you* do instead? WWYD?

Let's walk through an example.

My client Paul always ends up pulling away in intimate relationships. He has the belief that everyone always leaves, so at the first sign of any problem he starts distancing himself from the relationship to protect himself from what he sees as the inevitable ending. Of course his behavior proves his theory. Everyone *does* leave him but not because they would have on their own—it's because he freaks out and pulls away.

Paul's task was to figure out what he wanted to do instead of pull away. Paul asked himself, "If I wasn't a slave to this pattern, what would I do (WWID)?" Because he has enough awareness of the pattern to recognize it early, he can now notice himself beginning to pull away, and step in and reroute when he feels it coming on. As soon as he feels himself starting to pull away in a relationship, he can switch to what he'd rather do.

With my help, Paul decided that what he'd really like to do instead of pull away is to sit with the fear and vulnerability that comes up when he feels like someone is about to leave. He wanted to take a deep breath in that moment and remind himself that this was just an old pattern replaying and no immediate action was needed on his part. He wanted to remind himself that this person he feared leaving was not necessarily out the door, and that his current relationship was different from past relationships.

He visualized himself sitting with the fear and vulnerability until they passed. He saw himself not acting until he could take action that didn't feel defensive. He wanted to feel comfortable reaching out to the person he was afraid would leave. Instead of pulling away in fear, he saw himself reaching out to the other person to address his fears head on.

Paul got really clear on how these new actions would look and feel. He imagined himself doing them over and over, mentally practicing his new way of being. None of these things would be natural or easy. He knew that. In fact, they all felt extremely hard.

But that's the point. What you choose to do instead will usually be the complete opposite of your natural responses. It's going to feel foreign and uncomfortable. If it didn't, you would have been doing these things all along.

You can feel uncomfortable and take the new path anyway. I know you can. The more practice you have with the new actions, the easier they are.

If you weren't a slave to your pattern, what would you do (WWYD)?

15

Resistance and Change: Why Things Get Worse Before They Get Better

When you are embarking on growth or change, there's a massive force holding you back.

I'm not talking about the way your brain becomes programmed in certain ways and it takes some momentum to push through the habitual, routine response in order to reprogram old habits that may be holding you back.

I'm not talking about the people in your life who are afraid of you changing because of what it means for them, although they'll be there too. For some people, your change means their need to change so they're going to fight back.

Although all those obstacles will come up, there's a more basic form of resistance.

Sometimes it feels like fear. It *often* feels like fear.

Sometimes it feels like uncertainty. Suddenly you are not sure what to do next.

Sometimes it feels like doubt. Wait a minute…am I *sure* I want to make this change?

Whatever specific form it takes, it's a whopping feeling of opposition. It feels like a massive boulder has just been dropped in your path. Guess what? It's part of the process. Please re-read that last line. The monster resistance you are experiencing right before a big change is totally normal.

It's just what happens. And actually, the bigger your change and the more important it is to you, the stronger the resistance will be. The mind doesn't like change. The mind likes efficiency and for things to be familiar and predictable.

The ego *really* doesn't like change. The ego's life is threatened when you go around improving yourself, evolving, and taking chances. Ego would love for you to stay very small and dependent on it. When you're not, it's out of a job.

Take my client Rebecca. Her ego convinced her long ago that she was best off doing what other people wanted for her. She should work in a highly respected career with a great income, although she hated it. What she really wanted to do was be a life coach, but that was too socially unacceptable.

When she finally took the leap from living for "everyone" to living for herself—which she only did when the stress of being in a job she hated started making her physically ill—her ego didn't make it easy on her.

That's an understatement.

Her ego resisted at every point along the way. She was paralyzed with fear while taking her coach training course. She was plagued by writer's block and anxiety when she tried to write copy for her first website. She clammed up and her mind went blank on her first few client calls. She was getting a huge dose of resistance; maybe more than most because this change was so important to her.

Most people would turn back after the first or second road block. They would say, "It must not be meant to be. If this change were meant to be, it would be easy."

I say, "Where in the world did you get that idea?"

Because everything I've ever learned says just the opposite. Big change gives you big challenges. The bigger the challenges the more you get to prove yourself. Resistance floods in when the stakes are high because when the stakes are low, who cares? The ego isn't scared. There's nothing at stake and nothing to fear. Instead of telling yourself that obstacles are a sign that you are off course, and instead of turning back at the first bump, forge ahead. See the resistance as a sign that you are *on course* and keep going, even when it feels treacherous.

Feel the resistance and make your change anyway. Turning back at the road blocks only gives the *illusion* of safety. It's not actual safety. Safety is always found in following your right path.

16

A Story About Resistance

Five months into my relationship with my now-husband, I flaked and tried to bail. It was a textbook ego-resistance move.

I knew this relationship was for real and I got scared. Or, I should say, my ego knew it was for real and got scared for her little ego life. Ego knew she was facing extinction in her favorite playground—relationships. So as egos do, she cashed in with one huge last-ditch effort.

Hubby (then boyfriend) and I were having breakfast at Village Deli in Bloomington. They have the best breakfast. I had blueberry pancakes and he had an omelet. We were discussing a visit to go see his family for the following weekend. Most of the plans had been made, but we were talking about the details over breakfast. It would be the first time I would be meeting his family and there was a lot of hype about our trip.

He was a little nervous, but excited to take me home. He was really cute, doing and saying everything right, giving me the low-down on everyone I'd meet, and reassuring me that they'd love me. I couldn't hear the great things he was saying because of one phrase that kept screaming in my head.

"It's too much. It's too much. I can't handle this right now."

Not "It's wrong," (it wasn't). Not, "He's not right for you," (he clearly was). Just, "It's too much."

It *was* too much.

The relationship was too supportive, too healthy. I had too much to lose. I felt too vulnerable. He was too kind and he made it feel too simple. All of those "too much" fears slammed up against my deeply held beliefs like, "Relationships are hard," "If it seems too good to be true, it is," and "This isn't the way relationships work for me."

This relationship felt so good but also was so completely foreign that I couldn't see straight. One moment I'd thank my lucky stars and relax into appreciating what had come my way, and the next I'd deny that it was possible and totally convince myself that he wasn't for real. I knew he'd do something to show his true colors, eventually.

I had never *seen* a relationship like this one, let alone actually been *in* one. I knew power struggles and fighting. I believed that relationships either end after the honeymoon period or both parties eventually settle for much less than what they really want. Other than relationships on television shows, I literally never, ever saw it any other way.

I usually fell for married men. They had something to lose, and I reasoned that if they wanted to be with me, it meant I was worth taking a risk for. I set it up so that only unavailable men could prove they cared. Nothing short of risking a marriage registered with me as genuine caring.

I was always waiting for the other shoe to drop; in constant fear that as soon as I got comfortable in a relationship something would abruptly change. That was my pattern—it was how I spent my childhood, always on guard against the next life-changing event that I couldn't control. I couldn't let myself get comfortable or I'd really end up screwed.

And man, I could spin *anything* into a problem. He told me he loved me too soon…must mean he's needy. He wasn't a jealous jerk when I'd go out with girlfriends or talk about my male friends…must mean he doesn't care enough. If you look for a problem, you'll find one.

Despite all that I had been through in previous relationships, my inner voice urged me all along that *this* relationship was the real thing. From the beginning, it felt guided. Things fell into place easily and effortlessly. As much as my ego wanted to discount all of that, I couldn't completely quiet the still, small voice. So that morning at Village Deli, my ego hit its tipping point. It freaked the hell out that I might actually end up in an easy relationship with a nice, available guy.

The "This is too much, I can't handle this right now," that was echoing in my head drove me to cry all over my blueberry pancakes. I spent most of breakfast in the bathroom while my boyfriend sat at the table, stunned and clueless. One minute we were talking about what to pack for our trip, and the next minute I was saying, "I can't do this."

He drove me home. I remember sitting in his car in front of my house, and him, shell-shocked, asking, "Do you want to break up?" I said I didn't know. I really didn't. I had no idea. He was on his way to work a twelve-hour shift and would come over that night if I wanted him to. I decided I had twelve hours to get my act together.

I told myself I would *not* put this innocent guy through my crap—I was going to give him an answer in twelve hours, either way. He didn't come from divorce, guilt trips, and serial monogamy like I had. He didn't understand why I was making the situation so hard. He didn't understand that hard was familiar, so in many ways hard was easy for me.

The clock was ticking so I went straight to the spiritual masters for guidance. Marianne Williamson's *A Return to Love* was up first. It had saved me before and I had faith it could save me again. I re-read all my highlighted sections. I hit my knees and prayed, just like the book prescribed. I meditated. I cried. I got seriously pissed at my ego which was taunting me the whole time: "You knew this day would come. It's inevitable. Just walk away, normal relationships aren't for you."

Finally, I threw in the towel. On my knees, I handed it all over to whatever power was bigger than ego. I totally surrendered and begged for a miracle.

Then I took a long nap.

I woke up feeling more peaceful, but still not sure of what to do. The ego voice had quieted some. I asked that Spirit trump ego and continue to guide me. That seemed to be happening, given the relatively quiet state of my ego. In peace, I sat and listened. Doing nothing felt extremely awkward and like a giant waste of time, but I did it anyway. I sat on my bed and just listened.

I thought of my former therapist, a man whom I adored. I suddenly remembered some advice he once gave me. We were talking about my tendency to get bored in relationships when the guy is available. Give me a man I couldn't have and I'd never get bored; but one with an open calendar and I had the urge to run after few months. My therapist suggested that the next time I feel the urge to bolt, I stick around a little longer. Even though it wouldn't feel natural, he suggested that I commit to hanging out for another week or another month in order to break through that sticking point and see what was on the other side.

That was it. Although the solution to my momentous problem—the way that conversation just drifted into my mind—seemed much too random and unmonumental that was the miracle I needed. I didn't need a bolt of lightening or an earth shattering realization. I simply needed to remember an old conversation.

So I decided to do nothing about my relationship. When the "It's too much" ego voice piped up, I ask for Spirit to guide me instead of ego. I'd acknowledge that ego voice and keep hanging on, in spite of it. I chose to trust that if this really wasn't the relationship for me, I'd know that with clarity. I wouldn't leave out of fear. If I was going to leave someday it would be out of love, with the clear knowledge that something better was waiting.

I'd wait it out because I believed my therapist and Marianne Williamson and every other source I trusted in the world were all saying the same thing: this was nothing more than ego resistance. Ego had no place in this relationship and was afraid of its extinction. Ego was fighting for its life.

What I really want you to understand is that sticking it out didn't suddenly feel easy or like freedom. The *choice* was clear, but the *daily action* was not easy. Ego didn't vanish, I simply chose to hear it and continue on in spite of it. I stopped *listening to* its warnings and *obeying* its commands, but they didn't go away. The decision to stick it out was nothing more than a series of choices. I decided what I wanted to do and then did it even when ego was screaming at me to run.

Afterword

That night, when he came over I came clean. I confessed everything, but I continued to vacillate between moments of comfort and moments of sheer panic, having the urge to run and, oddly enough, missing the familiar feeling of being alone. I did meet his family that weekend and although my ego was still trying to crash the party, I also felt like I was exactly where I was supposed to be. I continued to own up to my fears regularly throughout our entire relationship. Exposing the ego is the fastest way to shut it down. It's like pouring water on a fire.

He helped me, too. This kind, logical man from an intact family wasn't about to let me give into ego and ruin what we had and he told me so. He was willing to help me see through ego's crap. He demanded it, actually.

And yes, we are living happily ever after.

But if I had let ego run the show that morning I wouldn't have spent the last eight years with this man who is not perfect—but perfect for me. Instead, I asked for a miracle and I got it. Then I did the work every day after that to continue making the choice I knew was right—even when it didn't feel like the easy choice—until one day it *was* the easy choice.

17

Practice for Change

Changing patterns is achievable. You can definitely do it. But, it takes practice.

They say it takes 10,000 hours of deep practice to become an expert at something. Deep practice is a little different than regular practice. Deep practice is the focused and deliberate rehearsal of a new behavior. Feedback is typically available. The new behaviors you are practicing are repetitive and purposeful. There is usually an explicit goal of learning something new or forming a new habit.

With deep practice, you can change pretty much anything about yourself. Any unwanted pattern can be replaced with something better.

With 10,000 hours of deep practice, your brain is rewired. Change takes hold. What once felt foreign and unnatural becomes familiar and natural. Patterns that were once default and automatic are replaced with whatever you choose to practice instead.

Ten thousand hours is a lot of time. That's eight hours a day, seven days a week, for about three-and-a-half years. But here's the good news: you start seeing benefits long before you hit the 10,000 hour mark.

Your brain is rewiring each time you enact change. Each time you catch a pattern and stop it mid-cycle, or interrupt the automatic chain of events, or tap into the bigger picture of what you want activates change in your brain and those changes snowball.

And it changes you and your patterns forever.

So the 10,000 hour thing isn't as daunting as it may sound. Only three-and-a-half years of repetition and you are done, but…you'll see change much, much sooner than that. Each change is infinitely easier than the last and the effects build on each other quickly.

That's very good news.

Part II

Head and Heart

"Pain is inevitable. Suffering is optional.
—Buddhist proverb

This section is about thoughts and emotions—the sources of our greatest pleasure and our greatest suffering.

I was raised to value my thoughts, weren't you? I was encouraged to, "think things through" and "use your head." I assumed that the persistent thoughts that ran through my mind were all valid and true. How could they not be? They sounded like me. I always had lots of evidence to back them up. They sure *felt* true. No one ever told me I didn't have to take that mind chatter as truth. I bet no one every told you, either.

The Modern Enlightenment way to handle thoughts is to approach them with curiosity. When they're running around up there in your head, inquire into their nature. Ask yourself if they serve you. Be curious, not rigid.

You may not realize it, but you get to choose whether you really engage with a thought or not. It's up to you whether you take it out to play and give it life and credibility. Or whether you let it float through your mind and leave as gently as it entered with no special attention or fanfare.

As life coach Michael Neill says, "It's not that you keep meeting the wrong guys; it's that you keep sleeping with them." It's not that the unhelpful thoughts are there; it's that you engage with them.

What's the harm in blindly believing all our thoughts? One reason: our thoughts produce our emotions.

And emotions can feel as scary and meaningful as thoughts. We're afraid of negative emotions. We think they'll consume us or overwhelm us...or at least ruin our day. We treat emotions the same way we treat thoughts, as if we're victims of them, they strike from nowhere, and have power over us.

But that's only true when we fight and deny our emotions. When we resist them and try to hold them back they stick around and grow and they *do* seem to hurt. They seem never-ending and beyond our control.

The Modern Enlightenment way to deal with emotions is to feel them. Make room for them. Sit with them until they're done doing the little emotion dance they do.

When you allow yourself to really feel a big, bad emotion, it goes away because it realizes you are not intimidated. You are not going to take any crap so it need not hang out threatening and bullying you.

You feel it, it passes, and you move on. That's the Modern Enlightenment way. And that's what you are going to read about in the following chapters.

18

Check Your Head

For years, my mind went to the exact same place every morning during my workout. Unfortunately, it wasn't a place I wanted it to go.

My morning routine triggered thoughts about an unpleasant situation with a family member. Right around the time I'd break a sweat, there it was. Just like it had been the day before. If I let my mind do its thing, it would play this family drama all the way through. It replayed old conversations and imagined future conversations. It justified and rationalized my side of the story. Left unchecked, my mind would basically replay the same imaginary argument with itself every single day.

That's *not* how I wanted to start my day.

The busier our world gets and the more options surround us, the more our minds rely on common and familiar thought patterns. Those mental "ruts" are the path of least resistance. Automatic, default habits make us more efficient and faster. They save mental energy.

Our minds love habit and familiarity and this can operate to our advantage as well as to our detriment. If left unchecked, I'd spend the first forty minutes of my day focusing on something that made me feel awful. But there was another choice—noticing the natural direction my mind took and refocusing it so it would steer clear of those habitual ruts. With a little practice, I learned to harness that early morning mental juice and use it to my advantage.

It took two steps:

1. Noticing. Noticing is generally pretty easy once you get used to paying attention to the thoughts that inhabit your mind. Practice paying attention. Observe. Be a witness to your mental dialogue. To do this well, you have to keep your ego out of it. Observe non-judgmentally and maintain an uninvolved, outside perspective.

2. Refocusing. Refocusing simply means shifting your attention to what you'd rather think about. You can use the unwanted thoughts as a cue—each time my mind would wander to the family story again, I used those thoughts as a reminder to refocus.

The only tricky part to the refocusing step is that you may need to do it a few thousand times until your replacement thoughts become a habit. But even when progress feels slow, the process gets easier each day as your brain forms new default pathways.

And, *voilá*. Before you know it, your workout triggers thoughts that work *for* you rather than *against* you. It doesn't get better than that.

19

Shred the File

"Children are happy because they don't have a file in their minds called 'All the Things That Could Go Wrong.'"

—Marianne Williamson

Do you remember what life was like before *you* had a file called "All the Things That Could Go Wrong"?

Do you remember what it was like to wake up without a care in the world? Can you think back to a time before the mental tape started broadcasting your to-do list, or revisiting the memory of that thing you screwed up, or offered predictions of what might go horribly wrong that day? Depending on your childhood, you may actually remember this time. Or your file may have been created earlier than most and you might not remember ever feeling totally free and not weighed down with worry.

It doesn't matter now. You can get it *back* if you once had it, or you can *get it* for the first time now. Yes now, as an adult. Really, you can. The tape won't necessarily shut off for long, but that doesn't matter either.

Sporadic moments of being free from the running tape are bliss. It's *so* worth working toward.

Here are some of my favorite ways of pausing the tape or shredding the 'All the Things That Could Go Wrong' file. These tools are based on Stephen Hayes' Acceptance and Commitment Therapy (ACT) and are described in the book *The Happiness Trap* by Russ Harris.

1. Know what your file says. Write down every "OMG, X could go wrong" thought you have over the course of a week. (Extra credit: read over the list and have a good laugh at yourself.)

2. Name those could-go-wrong stories. Maybe you have a good I-could-run-out-of-money story. Or you tell a whopper of a what-if-I-get-cancer story. Or perhaps you are a my-husband-is-going-to-leave-me-and-my-kids-will-hate-me kind of gal. Naming your stories highlights how predictable and habitual they are and it helps you to distance yourself from them. You will begin to see that when the I-suck-at-my-career story starts playing, it's not personal. It's not real. It's just a groove in the record that's so deep it's difficult to erase.

3. Remember that none of these stories mean anything unless you make them mean something. They are empty and meaningless in and of themselves. Any sting they have is only because you are choosing to believe them. They aren't facts. They aren't real. The tape starts automatically—the file runs without your permission—but no one said you have to pay attention.

4. One last tip, just for fun: Change the voice. Try telling your No-one-loves-me-and-I'll-always-be-alone story in a Mickey Mouse voice. Or say it the way Yoda would say it: "Loved not am I and always alone will I be."

Now how serious does it sound?

20

Peeling Back the Layers

"I decided to start anew, to strip away what I had been taught."
—Georgia O'Keefe

We don't see the world as it is, we see it as we are. We see it through layers of stuff. Stuff like beliefs, fears, memories, opinions, and ideas about what we think will make us happy.

Those layers pile on top of each other and bury our core self. You know, the core 'you' that was there when you a little kid, dancing around in your underwear, not caring how you looked in your underwear or that you had no rhythm. The core is still there; it's always there…it's just buried under your layers.

The layers—beliefs and opinions and such—are like glasses you might wear. You can't help but see everything through the glasses that are firmly planted on your face. After a while you forget you are wearing glasses at all, until it rains and you get some raindrops on your lenses. Out of nowhere you are reminded there's a filter there. Something artificial is distorting your view.

How do you peel back the layers so you can reach the core?

I'd like to share my practice for peeling back the layers. I teach this practice to all of my clients. The first crystal clear indication that I'm filtering the world through a bunch of stuff that's not serving me is a vague, indefinable feeling of ick. So I write down every thought that's running through my mind. Every one I can catch and nail down, anyway. (It gets easier as you go.)

It's like doing a brain dump of everything that's running through my head. It's important to get the thoughts out, by writing them down. You can't mentally run through the thoughts because as they keep swirling around in your mind they pick up steam. It's only when you get them out on paper that they loosen their grip on you.

Then, I look through the list of painful beliefs with an open mind.

With an open mind and no attachment, I play devil's advocate and try to see which of my painful beliefs might not be 100 percent true. That usually includes all of them.

Examining the belief, "I'll never make it to the end," allows me to ask, "How might I make it to the end?" Then I think of how. When I write, "She doesn't care about me," I can turn it on its head with: "Maybe she does care." Then I find concrete evidence—real world examples—of her caring.

This exercise shows me how I may have jumped to conclusions. How maybe—just maybe—there's another possibility to the thoughts that I am quick to believe just because they've been around for a while.

On a really good day, I come up with replacement thoughts I can think instead. Like this morning, I decided to replace, "I'm not doing enough in my business," with, "I made up the rules for 'enough' and actually, I'm doing pretty well." I find evidence to support my replacement thought, such as all the work I did last week.

I also decided to replace, "I have way too much to do," with, "I'll do as much as I can and the world will not fall apart. None of these tasks are as important as my ego is telling me they are." That new thought feels really good and I know it's at least as true as the original thought. Particularly since the original thought wasn't helping me.

By doing this, I peel back a layer or two and I'm closer to my core. I may not be dancing in my underwear yet, but I'm almost there. I believe fewer stories. And there are moments I'm fully aware of the glasses at the end of my nose.

21

Change the Channel

I have conflicting feelings about television.

Of course there's nothing inherently bad about TV. The problem is that it's so easy to cross that line from fun-and-entertaining-diversion to tool-used-to-disengage-from-life. The issue is, when the TV's always on, someone else is doing your thinking for you. If you let it run from *The Today Show* to *The Tonight Show*, when do you get to hear what you have to say?

Many people have the TV on from *Today* to *Tonight*. They also tend to be the same people who pay me their hard-earned money to help them figure out what to do with their lives. They aren't sure what they like, what they're passionate about, or what gets them excited. They have the sense that they're wasting time. They say they're not sure who they really are. I say it's no wonder, because they don't spend any time with themselves. They know Matt Lauer and Jay Leno better than they know themselves.

And listen, no judgment. Seriously. We all have ways of disengaging, numbing, or escaping from time to time. In my life, I've used everything from too much work to too much wine to take a break from the present moment. So I'm not judging.

It's just that TV slips in there because it's so acceptable. It's so common. And it's so harmless, right? Well, it could definitely be worse. But when you are getting really honest with yourself, identifying your patterns, and working on your issues because you know you deserve the most joyful and authentic life you can have, "it could be worse" just isn't good enough.

Our ability to create new thought is the best thing ever and we create our lives with our thoughts. Want to become a nurse? You use your thoughts and your imagination to see the path to that goal. First, you see the steps required to doing it in your mind. You see yourself the way you'd be as a nurse so that when you are there, you will recognize it and know what to do next.

Want to find a happy relationship? You focus on happy relationships around you, take pieces of what you've seen and experienced and create your own image in your mind so that when the right partner shows up, you recognize him.

If you are never silent—if you never generate your own thoughts— you are simply reacting to other people's thoughts. You are living a life of reaction, not creation. You just take what you get and deal with it.

I know that's not what you want. Creating is much too fun to settle for anything less.

And to create, you have to turn off the TV and listen to what you have to say once and a while.

22

The Whole Picture?
Or Mentally Myopic?

Things often seem really dire when you are up close.

Like when you are pregnant, sweaty, and starving and you think your husband looked a little too long at a hot, un-pregnant woman on the street. When you accuse him of not loving you anymore, you are looking at the situation from too close up. It's like observing a Monet from inches away: you don't get the whole picture. Things are fuzzy and you draw wacky conclusions when you focus on the parts and don't take in the whole image.

This also happens when you get an idea in your head and you replay it over and over, ignoring everything else. Including the truth.

Maybe you need a new dress for the wedding next weekend. Must Have It. Must Go Shop Now. It feels so important that you literally don't see all the other dresses hanging in your closest. You can't see that it's time to work, not shop. You are not seeing the whole picture—you are nose-to-the-Monet about the damn dress.

Is there a solution for being mentally myopic?

When something has such a grip on you that it's all you can see, you can usually feel yourself there. Step one...stop. Don't act on it. Acting on it always makes it worse. Don't scream at your husband. Give yourself permission to do it in five minutes—the delay will serve you well. Drop your car keys. Give yourself permission to shop later. Step two...step back. Way back. Look around. Use your peripheral vision, literally and metaphorically.

One of my mentors calls it "soft focus". Don't home in on anything; instead, relax your focus and take in as much as you can. See the whole scene and give yourself a minute to breathe, relax, and detach from the situation.

Soft focus is the way a cat looks when she's lying in the sun. Her eyes are barely open, lazy and relaxed, soft, just gazing around, not fixed on anything.

When you are mentally myopic, take a step back and be the cat. If you are still driven to act on your idea in five minutes or five days, act on it. But you probably won't be. Being the cat works wonders when it comes to seeing what's really at hand.

23

Look Away...is
Your Problem Still There?

Think of a problem you have. Now ask yourself, would this problem still exist if I stopped thinking about it? (I heard this from Supercoach and radio host Michael Neill. I have such a huge mind crush on this guy it's not even funny.)

Go ahead, try it.

Real problems remain, even when you stop thinking about them. In fact, real problems grow when you try to put them out of your mind. But problems of the ego mind, which are based in fear, require your focus in order to survive. These are not real problems; they are figments of your imagination. So when you look away, they go away. When you stop thinking about them, they usually begin to disappear.

I know, I wasn't convinced at first either. So I suspended my disbelief and tried it.

Problem: I need a root canal.

Wait...stop thinking about it....shift my focus to something else....
the problem is still there. And it's getting worse by the minute. It must be
a real problem that shouldn't be ignored.

Problem: My friend is annoying me with her negativity and
complaining.

Wait...stop thinking about it....shift my focus to something else...
gone. It wasn't a real problem that required my attention. It was a problem in my mind, but there was nothing required of me to solve it in the
physical world.

Problem: A woman is raped every minute in The Congo.

Wait...stop thinking about it....shift my focus to something else....
the problem is still there. And it's getting worse by the minute. It must be
a real problem that shouldn't be ignored.

Problem: I'm bored.

Wait...stop thinking about it....shift my focus to something else ...
gone. Something pops up to take its place and I forget about my boredom,
so it wasn't a real problem. It was only a problem of perception.

I could have turned my boredom into an existential crisis as I have
many times before, but instead I just waited. It turns out; the crisis would
have been for nothing.

Ask yourself: Would my problem still exist if I stopped thinking about
it? Then shift your focus and see what happens. It'll either go away or get
worse. Then you will have your answer.

24

Be Like Water

Want some suffering-repellent?

Be like water. That's how Wayne Dyer puts it. Be fluid and easy and fill in the cracks; don't be firm and rigid and unmoving.

Learn to yield.

Don't concretize and solidify your thoughts. That's how Tibetan nun and author Pema Chodron puts it. Soften around your thoughts, don't harden around them.

Be soft.

The ego hates soft and yielding and fluid. Egos love, love, love solid and concrete.

The ego wants to concretize things because we think it makes us feel better. We think we will get a resolution that way.

The other night, I wanted more than anything to have a quiet, relaxing evening. I wanted to read my book, light candles, and wear a Snuggie (I don't actually own a Snuggie, but it was that kind of night). Quiet, peace, candle-light, and a good book. But I don't live alone so I don't always get what I want. Hubby's not a fan of quiet book nights. He's a fan of bright lights and TV surround sound.

I could have created my quiet space in another area of the house but I didn't. Instead, I got all rigid about it. Thoughts like, "This is my house, too," "It's not fair," "We're so different," swam across my mind, as they always will. But instead of letting them swim along all fluid-like and continue on their way, I stopped them and turned them into concrete. I solidified them. I puffed them up and made them true and important.

When we went to bed and I started arguing my case about our home being too loud and not peaceful and how there's not enough compromise, my ego kept going and going. As if the more concrete I could make my argument and the more I could solidify my point, the better I'd feel, and the more resolution there would be.

Except that the opposite is true. Solidifying my point was digging my own grave. The really ironic and totally predictable part of the whole thing is that the thoughts my ego was solidifying into place—that our house was loud and not peaceful and there's no middle ground—were being so perfectly demonstrated by me in that moment. I was loud. I was not peaceful and I was not compromising.

On some level, we're always guilty of the things we accuse others of. Sometimes it's blatantly obvious like in this example, other times it's more subtle. But it's always there if you look.

The solution is to use suffering-repellent: Be soft and fluid, like water. Soften, don't harden around those thoughts swimming around in your mind. I could have let go of the judgments of my hubby and found peace. So can you.

25

Distinguish True
Intuition from Ego-Mind-Chatter

You feel an inner nudge. There's a voice. But can you trust it? How do you know? Is it really the deep voice of intuition, or only the shallow voice of the mind? Are you hearing the guidance of Truth or ego chattering away?

Here are some of the rules I use to determine the difference:

1. The real still, small voice within doesn't think you suck.
This is the numero uno best guideline ever. If the voice is saying, "You'll never make it as a ballerina because you lack discipline and talent and it's way too hard for someone like you," you can be pretty sure that's not your true, inner guidance speaking. Basically, your inner guidance doesn't sound like a jerk.

If the voice is bashing you, putting you down, or blowing things up just to scare you in any way, it's not real. That's not the voice you want to be listening for. If becoming a ballerina is not in your highest good, the inner voice of intuition might guide you toward other opportunities. You might hear a nudge to, "Keep pursuing other options," or "Do yoga today instead." Or you might simply gradually lose interest in ballet. However, your real inner guidance won't shame you away from it.

A Course in Miracles says there is only love or fear. Of those, only one is real (and it ain't fear). So if the voice sounds like love, listen up. If not, you can thank it for sharing and move along.

2. Truth has an undercurrent of peace.

Truth has a quality of peace to it—even when the Truth is not what you want to hear.

If the inner voice is saying your stomach problems go beyond simply having too much Mexican food, and the doctors and test results confirm that, you'll find a sense of peace. It's too bad that you are sick—it's not necessarily the answer you hoped for—but now you know the Truth.

If you suspect a friend is lying to you and she really is, there's a sense of peace when she confesses. Although it's not the reality you wanted, it usually hurts more to avoid and deny than to know.

If the voice is not speaking the Truth that sense of peace doesn't exist. When your mind is saying you failed at marriage, and you failed at business, and you practically failed at life, there's no peace because it's all a big lie.

But when your inner voice says your marriage as you know it is over, and your business as you know it is over, and they really are, there will be peace. You will experience hurt and sadness; uncertainty and fear, but also peace.

I heard this guideline for sorting out Truth versus Not Truth. It helps. If you are standing on a high dive board about to plunge into the water below, you are probably going to feel some fear and apprehension. Imagine you are diving into crystal clear, clean, safe water. That's what it feels like when you are doing the thing that's right for you but you're scared anyway. That's how Truth feels.

If you look down and realize you are about to plunge into dirty, toxic water, that's how it feels when it's not the right thing for you. That feeling is Not Truth.

3. Fear has urgency. Truth is patient.

When your thoughts feel rushed and urgent, that's a good sign that ego is taking over. When they're calm and patient, that's the peace of Truth shining through.

When I thought about writing this book, I felt some nervous excitement. I usually (although not always) felt motivated to take some action. Despite the endless self-doubt and fear, small action steps felt more like inspired action than forced action. Something in me knew it would happen. My inner guidance told me it would all come together, so there wasn't that sense of urgency around it. When I thought about finding a publisher, I felt the kind of urgency that grips your stomach and says it should have been done yesterday. No waiting until morning, no inspiration, it needs to be done, like, NOW.

That's not real. That's ego mind stuff and it often means your desire is rooted in fear. Ego desires typically look like avoiding a fearful outcome. In this case, ego desires are an attempt to avoid the horrible fate of writing my book for nothing, no one ever reading it, wasting my time, and disappointing myself. (None of which are even possible, by the way. Those are all dramatic ego-based fears that my mind told me could be avoided by finding the "right" publisher, right now).

Truth is patient because it's not avoiding anything, it's approaching something good. It's our true self moving toward what's right, not running from false pain. It's a sure bet. Because it's the right path, there's no need for it to be done by noon today. It will happen because it's meant to happen, there's no rush.

26

Awake, Aware, and Mindful

True story: One of my clients recently told me that the only memory he has of traveling between home and work last week was when he almost stepped on a dead rat. He couldn't remember a single detail of the other nine commutes—he was on total autopilot while he was up in his head, somewhere else—until the rat showed up on his path and brought him into the present moment.

This is not uncommon. And it's kind of sad because it was really nice outside last week. He would have enjoyed those moments of walking in the sunshine, noticing the people around him, and feeling how good his body felt to be moving.

But instead of being on those walks, he was focusing on next week trying to predict how his date might go. Then he jumped back to last week, reliving the humiliating staff meeting. Then he was in after work making his grocery list, then in last night, regretting his third glass of wine.

Then, because he was busy visiting places he didn't particularly want to be and he wasn't really experiencing his life as he lived it, he went through the week feeling dissatisfied and unfulfilled. Like there was more to life, he was missing something. Yeah, in fact, he's missing *everything*. Well, everything except the rat.

I do that too, don't you? I catch myself counting, planning, rehearsing, and thinking instead of being present in the moment. Mental busyness is one way to avoid the anxiety that sometimes comes with stillness. It's also a habit, an automatic pattern of being overly cerebral that will run on its own if we do nothing to stop it.

Here are a few things you can do to stop the mental gymnastics that keep you jumping away from the present:

- Focus on your breath. Feel it going in and out. Put your full attention on the air coming into and exiting your body.
- Ground yourself in your body. You can do this by studying the physical sensations in your hands or feet. Inhabit your body and really feel the sensations.
- Name things. Look around your immediate environment and name what you see. Black wooden chair, pink sparkle boots, iron curtain rod. Your focus will shift to what's right in front of you right now.

Once you are grounded in the present moment either through your breath or body or environment, try observing the random thoughts that pass through your mind. Don't judge anything or try to change any of it. Just observe.

Or bring full perceptual awareness to everything around you. Experience your senses to their max. You can use mindfulness in the shower, experiencing how the water feels and how your body is positioned. On a walk you can be aware of how the ground feels under your feet, hear the birds, and see the leaves hanging from the trees.

And there you have it—you are now officially mindful. You are tapped in, present, and here now. Enjoy real life.

27

Much More to Presence

Mindfulness is what you practice to cultivate presence. Presence is the state of being totally immersed in what's right in front of you. When you are present, worry and fear fall away because worry and fear do not exist in the now. They are memories of the past or projections into the imaginary future. They have nothing to do with what is happening right this second.

But there's even more to presence than watching worry melt away.

Have you noticed what else happens when you are totally present in the moment? If you have, you know what I'm talking about.

It's nearly impossible to not fall in love with everything around you when you are with it in the now, and when your mental and physical attention is focused and here. There is no mental straying, just presence.

When you really look into someone's eyes and you are there completely, it can almost feel overwhelming. There's too much emotion, too much beauty, too much love.

That 'too much' is probably why we train ourselves away from it.

Every time I allow myself to be truly present with my daughter, or a stranger, or a beautiful tree, I can't breathe for a second and my eyes fill with tears. That's presence.

That's the feeling we usually numb ourselves against. It's disruptive, for sure. It's emotional and raw and real. It takes energy and courage to go there.

Remember the character Ricky in the movie *American Beauty*? He's the teenager who films everything around him because there is so much beauty in the world he doesn't want to miss any of it. While watching a video of a plastic bag swirling in the wind he says, "Sometimes there's so much beauty in the world I feel like I can't take it… and my heart is just going to cave in."

It's no coincidence that he's also a pot dealer who's always stoned. When you are present to it, the beauty can almost be too much. So we numb and distract ourselves by being busy or shopping or getting high.

So lean into it, don't leap. Don't go staring deep into everyone's eyes, just pick one person and be right there with them for a second or two. You'll see what I mean.

Or start slowly and pick one tree to admire and appreciate. Before you know it, you'll build up a tolerance for beauty.

28

You Are Out of Your Mind

Has anyone ever told you that you are out of your mind? If so, you might take it as a compliment.

I was recently training a group of really smart people to be life coaches. Intelligence can be a serious obstacle. Time and again, I watched these sharp and intuitive people make things so much harder than they needed to be by over-thinking just about everything. They were trying to *figure out* how to solve their clients' problem.

The problem with thinking and figuring out is that as soon as you flip into mental mode, you are not *here* and present with your client anymore. When you are up in your head you've left the building as far as the issue is concerned. You are no longer in the moment being guided—you are in your head thinking about guiding.

You might be wondering: isn't thinking good? Isn't it *necessary*? Don't we *need* to figure things out and think them through in order to do our best work?

Yes. And no.

There's a definite time and place for logic, reasoning, thinking, and figuring. At the same time, thinking too much—paying too much attention to the concepts floating around in your head—is how you can very quickly get in your own way.

Here's another example from my life.

When I'm e-coaching, I'll often quickly read through an email from a client before I'm ready to respond. I plan to respond in the morning but I might read it from my BlackBerry while I'm lying in bed before I go to sleep. I read the client's problem. Then I lay there in bed, being in my head with their problem. What should I say? How should I say it? Which approach will be most effective?

Sometimes I come up a little blank. I think I'm not sure. I think I don't know what to say. I *think* a lot. Until I wake up, open the email and stop thinking. The minute I drop out of my head (which for me, coincides with beginning to type) everything comes together. The ideas, the words, and the help my client needs—the exact way to say something so that they hear it—feels like it's coming *through* me, not from me.

It's really kind of trippy. It's also really awesome.

Don't get me wrong, I'm not channeling some external source that knows all the answers. I'm tapping into what *I* know. I can tap in because my mind, with all its beliefs and fancy words, isn't getting in the way.

I'm quiet. Wordless. I'm able to lead because I just go where I'm led.

So when your thoughts are concept-based and verbal and fast and distracting, allow them to float by without engaging them. Shift your focus from those floating thoughts to what's right in front of you, mindfulness style.

Then be quiet and listen. You'll eventually hear your intuition. Remember, it's that still small voice that doesn't think you suck. It's the one that wants you to be quiet and stop drowning it out.

The one that knows almost everything you'll ever need to know.

29

How to Be a Big Baby

Have you ever watched a baby experience emotions?

Babies can't tell stories so their emotions are clean. They feel pure emotion without any narrative. If you take away a baby's favorite toy, they feel sad or angry or whatever they feel. "I want the toy and I don't have it so I'm sad." Period. They don't think, "This always happens to me and it probably always will and it's not fair. If I were cuter they wouldn't take my toys away."

When you add your narrative, the clean emotion of sadness gets tainted and it turns very dirty. It becomes a dirty blob of sadness plus shame plus resistance plus arguing with reality plus whatever else. That dirty blob is what a human adult might feel, but not a baby. Babies are too smart for that nonsense.

There are lots of benefits to doing it the baby way.

First, without a narrative you don't get the messy emotions like guilt and shame. Guilt and shame are totally narrative-based. Without a narrative, you get to stick with cleaner, more basic emotions like sadness and fear.

Second, you move through an unwanted emotion QUICKLY when you are not adding dirty pain to the mix. Babies feel what they feel, and they really feel it. When you allow yourself to feel what you feel, it gets to move through you in no time. Babies don't deny or resist how they feel the way adults do.

Babies don't know enough to distract themselves in hopes of dodging a negative emotion. They don't turn to online shopping or compulsively twitter or eat cake when they feel bad. They just feel bad. And soon, they don't feel bad. Because when you play it that way, feeling bad is over very quickly.

Seriously, watch a baby. As I've been writing this, I could hear my baby crying in the other room. She cried for about twenty seconds. Then there was silence for a minute or so. Then I heard her talking and laughing. It happens this way all the time. Babies can't tell stories that make emotions dirty. They can't resist emotions, so the emotions fly right by.

Maybe we should all act more like babies.

30

The Inclination to Bolt

I used to feel something quite a bit. I called it bored, although I knew that wasn't really it. Restless might have described it but it felt worse than restless. I was uncomfortable in my own skin. It felt like it was dangerous or really unpleasant to be me in that moment.

It was a restlessness that made me want to move, be busy, disassociate, or become numb. I felt it behind my eyes and my vision was unsteady. My heart rate increased, my breath became shallow, and my mind raced. Bored is the label I gave it because that label gave me an excuse to do something to avoid the feeling. When you are bored, you find something to do. Everyone knows that. Getting up and doing something was the exact opposite of how to best deal with that feeling, though.

Pema Chodron says, "Never underestimate the inclination to bolt." That was it, exactly. I wanted to bolt, so I lied to myself and said I was bored, giving myself permission to bolt. Bolting was a band-aid and not a very good one. Bolting sent the message that yes, this feeling is too big for you, and it's too uncomfortable. You can't handle it, Amy, RUN! Do what you can to not feel what its like to be you in this moment. Get away from yourself, numb, in any way you can. This reaction was not cool, because then numbing becomes the new pattern. Then the numbing takes on a life of its own and brings its own issues.

What was that feeling about? I had my theories, but it doesn't really matter. The way out is through. The feeling was a doorway. If I could sit with it, it would lose its power. Sit. Fight the inclination to bolt. Practicing what I preach. I tell my clients in that annoying broken record kind of way, "Every emotion has a beginning, middle, and end. If you sit with it and feel it all the way through, it passes faster than you think. It can't swallow you up or kill you. Feel it through to the end and the pressure stops building."

I like to use the beach ball analogy. I over-use it, I'm sure. "It's like holding a beach ball under water. You can do it for a while with sheer force, but as soon as you look away the ball flies up and smacks you in the face. It's the same with emotions. Feel them as they come up, let the ball rise to the surface instead of trying to hold it down, and the ball will eventually just float away."

I can see how hearing that again and again could sound annoying. I understand that it can be harder than I make it sound. But still, the message is right.

So I sat still. I fought the inclination to bolt. Practiced what I preached. And the feeling is mostly gone now. And I'm starting to really get what was behind it.

31

Can You Embrace Feeling Like Crap?

Where did we get the belief that we're supposed to always feel good? We're not. Feeling like crap once in a while makes our lives so much better. It provides contrast. It shows us what we don't want and motivates us to find what we do want. In nature there is chaos before clarity. The caterpillar dissolves into goo before it becomes a butterfly; the violent storm is followed by an almost eerie peace. The same is true for us.

If you are feeling especially lost, directionless or uninspired, that means something better is coming. In order to make a giant leap in your mindset or expand your identity, the old stuff has to come down. We have to walk through the ring of fire. It burns like hell, but sometimes you need to burn the barn down and start over instead of trying to fix the walls that are made of rotting wood.

The interesting thing about this burning down and starting over process is that it can be really painful if you let it, but it doesn't have to be. If you recognize it for what it is and know that it's leading you closer to the promised land, it's not so bad. It may not be comfortable, but it's not quite as scary.

Shifting perspectives is tiring emotional work. When you start making major changes in the way you see the world and what you believe, you are going to get tired. Sometimes you'll get sick. Both are actually excellent signs that what you are doing is working.

Retreat. Cocoon. Rest. Let yourself feel like crap and don't try to rush out of it or tell a story about it. Just hold on tight and know that even as your identity bursts into flames around you, the next step is rebuilding your barn.

And the next step after that is having a big barn dance to celebrate how much better the new barn is.

32

Skip to the Fun Part of Enlightenment

The Universe sent me a note the other day.

Here's what it said:

For millennia, Amy, the path to enlightenment has been made up of many steps. Most commonly, it begins with festering misunderstandings that lead to pain, the pain then leads to growth, growth leads to clarity, clarity leads to fun, fun leads to joy, and joy leads to true illumination.

May I recommend skipping to the fun part?

Love you forever, Amy,

The Universe

Do you get it?

This means all the misunderstandings, painful times, moments of sheer terror, feeling "stuck," thinking you are wasting your time that you are spinning your wheels and will most definitely never get "there", are a necessary part of the plan. The pain kicks the whole process into motion. The pain kicks growth into gear, and growth eventually trips the Enlightenment switch.

This is where most of us get stuck. We fight against the pain and refuse to feel it, so we don't grow organically. We curse the Universe and ourselves for not doing things Right, for not already being at Enlightenment (as if there's a there, there).

Because we're so focused on right and wrong and black and white we stay constricted and we shut down. Shut down, constricted, and clutching, is the opposite of how we need to be in order to grow. Growth requires a letting go. Growth doesn't just like letting go, it requires it. There must be some degree of turning things over and trusting in order for growth to happen.

What to do instead:

When you feel like you are in the wrong life or you've made some awful mistake or you just aren't good enough, say, "thank you." Thank those feelings of pain because their sole purpose is to help you grow. You don't grow when you are sitting there mindlessly eating popcorn and watching *The Real Housewives* of wherever. You grow through pain.

So thank it, and remember that the pain is just as important a step toward Enlightenment as joy and growth and clarity. It's sometimes less fun, but no less important.

Then let go. Allow the pain to work its magic and allow the growth to start. When you do that, you are in the fun part of the equation before you know it.

33

A Coaching Session About Fear

Below is an e-mail exchange between one of my clients and me. I share it with her full blessing, of course.

I'm using it here because her feelings are so common. They are so real and so human. I hear these same thoughts expressed all the time—in my own head and from the mouths of others.

Although she really believed her pain was unique, I finally convinced her that nearly everyone can relate to what she's going through. This is her real life—it's no artificial text-book example—and I'm inspired by her honesty and courage in allowing me to share it with you.

She's in the early stages of starting a business venture. Here's her e-mail to me:

Hi Amy,

I am freaking out a little...I am totally overwhelmed about pulling the trigger and starting this business. I am afraid that I don't know enough and won't be successful.

Afraid that I will let people down and look foolish. Afraid that I am biting off more than I can chew.

I have the biggest urge to hide and avoid everything.

I am so scared. I also am so broke and can't stop thinking about how I need to have more money. That too makes me want to crawl under a huge rock.

You've felt this way before, no? Here's my response to her:

Dear Beth,

Okay, stop. Take a deep breath. (Really, take a second to do it.)

You are fine. Your mind is moving very quickly telling you lots of lies, but they're not real. It's just the mind and the ego doing exactly what they do. There is no truth to the thoughts you are thinking. The only reason they're affecting you so much is because you are listening to and believing them.

You get to choose which thoughts you focus on and buy into and replay over and over. When a particular thought feels true to us, we embellish it. We fondle it and expand on it and make it seem very real and powerful. It's not. That's all that's going on here. The fear you feel is the consequence of elaborating on and believing those thoughts.

The only way anyone ever does anything new is by taking small steps that scare the crap out of them. I'm not kidding about this, not even a little bit.

You are at a point right now that every single human being who has ever done anything in life has visited. You can listen to the fears (lies) and choose to do what you want to do anyway, or you can listen to the fears and take them very seriously.

Most people take the second option. They're the same people who wake up at age seventy and wonder why they didn't take more chances in life.

You say: *I am totally overwhelmed about pulling the trigger and starting this business.*

There is no trigger to pull. That's just a picture your mind created and it's scaring you away, but it's a figment of your imagination. There is no trigger; there is no moment of starting a business. There's just the next small step, then the next, then the next. You can't snap your fingers or pull a trigger and have a business today; all you can do is talk to the next client, or make your business cards, or do whatever the next step is. You can't possibly do anything "wrong" because there is no right or wrong next step.

Send me your answers to the questions below so that we can work through them.

You say: *I am afraid that I don't know enough and won't be successful*.

Tell me what is so bad about trying something new and not being successful. What would it mean about you? (Obviously, it wouldn't actually mean anything. But you are telling yourself it would mean something. What's your story?)

How would you know if you were successful? You are defining "success"…how are you defining it? Tell me what success and failure look like at this point.

Tell me three ways in which you know more than enough to take the next small step in your business.

You say: *I'm afraid that I will let people down and look foolish*.

So what? Tell me what it would mean if someone felt let down because of your business choices.

How might you let people down if you don't take a chance? How might you let yourself down?

Who exactly is counting on you to make this business work?

You say: *I'm afraid that I am biting off more than I can chew*.

If you are afraid you are taking on more than you can handle, take on less. When you believe you have to take huge steps and have perfect success, you end up frozen by fear and you do nothing. Just do a little less until it doesn't feel so overwhelming.

You say: *I have the biggest urge to hide and avoid everything*.

Yup, that's normal. Sounds like you are right on track.

I felt that way yesterday when I met a millionaire business man for a six-hour, hard-core coaching session. He did a lot of searching for the best coach and he chose me.

The thoughts, "He's paying me too much," "I'm not good enough," "I might let him down," "I want to sneak out and go shopping," ran through my mind all day long. But I recognized those fears and called them what they were (ego lies) and I coached him the best I could for six hours straight anyway.

I hope he feels the benefits today, but that's not my business. I can't control how he feels and you can't control letting people down. All you can do is live your life and let them have their opinions. If they choose to feel let down, that's their prerogative. It's none of your business.

You say: *I am so scared.*

I know, sweetie. That's part of it, too. But you can do scared—you've handled much worse. You are also scared to not start the business, so you are "doing" scared either way, right?

Scared is how you feel but it has zero to do with how you choose to act.

You say: *I also am so broke and can't stop thinking about how I need to have more money. That too makes me want to crawl under a huge rock.*

"I need to have more money," and "I'm so broke," would make anyone want to crawl under a rock.

Your financial state is always in flux and it's always temporary. Is it definitely true that you need to have more money than what you have right now? You are making it work now with what you have…what makes you say you need more?

What are you afraid will happen? Now look at each fear you listed and think of at least three ways it won't happen.

What *do* you have? From where I sit, it looks like you have a lot of opportunity, a lot of intelligence, a lot of wisdom, experience, personality, support, and connections. Use those.

I know it's scary but scary isn't ever going to be obsolete. Scary is par for the course. I wish it were easier, but doing little things that scare you everyday is the only path to success I know. I KNOW you can hack it, you just have to choose it.

xo-A

34

Keep your Dreams Clean

"Your goals minus your doubts equal your reality."
        –Ralph Marston

Exactly.

In graduate school I studied the way information is mentally represented, and how concepts are stored, processed, and retrieved. I'm going to put that knowledge to use here because the way you mentally represent both your dreams and your doubts is important.

It says a lot about whether your doubts impact your dreams. Every dream comes with its own set of doubts. So while banishing all doubt isn't a reasonable objective, keeping your dream separate from your doubts is a brilliant idea and a very worthy goal.

Let's say you want to scale Kilimanjaro. Or win the Heisman Trophy. You have a lot of thoughts about your goal, many of which are very positive. You have your passion for the cause. You have nurtured your fantasies of making it to the top or hearing your name called as the winner. You are buoyed by the encouragement you've received from others. You have memories of having practiced your craft and done really well—moments when you are in the flow and success seems inevitable.

All of that mental content is gold. It gets you pumped up and fuels your passion. Spending time focusing on that cerebral ball of good stuff launches you straight toward success.

Of course, you also have some doubts. You have memories of practice sessions that didn't go so smoothly and that look you got from skeptics. There are flashbacks of the times you watched your competition outperform you on the field, or the image of the ground 1,000 feet below you that's burned into your mind. Your own doubts and fears will float in and out of your mind, oh…about a gazillion times a day. That's all perfectly human.

The trick is keeping your dream and your doubts separate so they can each be what they are and do what they do without your doubts bleeding all over your dreams. How do you keep them separate? Think of them independently and speak about them as independent and separate. Label your dream your dream, and your doubts your doubts.

Instead of saying, "I'd love to win the Heisman *but* I'm on a crappy team," which implies that the doubts (crappy team) have something to do with the dream (win the Heisman) say, "I'd love to win the Heisman. I also happen to be on a crappy team."

Being on a crappy team is a *perceived* obstacle but if you've learned anything in this book so far it's that perceptions aren't always accurate. You have doubts about your ability to win the Heisman and it may be a fact that your team is awful, but those don't necessarily negate your goal.

One thing is for sure: if you assume the team destroys your chances at the Heisman, it does. I can pretty much promise you that.

You have your dream of reaching the top of Mount Kilimanjaro, and then you have your doubts about not being able to do it without breaking your neck. So keep them separate. On the one hand, your training has shown you that you can scale large mountains with amazing skill and ease. On the other hand, you are scared. Both are fine, just keep them independent. The fear doesn't negate the dream. It actually doesn't mean anything about the dream—it just means you feel fear.

When you picture yourself falling to your death, remember that's just a scary image your mind created. Obviously let it inspire you to take precautions to avoid that outcome, but that doesn't mean replaying the fear over and over. It just requires taking safety seriously.

Once you've used the fear to prepare yourself the best you can, then it's time to filter out that fear when it comes around. Stash it away in the "doubts" box in your mind. See it, acknowledge it, and then store it in the "doubts" bin and put a lid on it. Don't let it play with anything in the "dream" bin.

The more you can think, "This is my dream *and* those are my doubts," rather than "This is my dream *but* these are my doubts," the cleaner and prettier your dream will be.

35

Do You Manufacture Worry?

It takes courage to be happy.

It's very human to worry about the uncertainty of life. It's normal to be afraid that all the good stuff you have is going to vanish and you won't be able to cope.

Researcher and author Brené Brown talks about the panic that sets in while she's staring lovingly at her sleeping children. Her thoughts race from, "Aren't they precious?" to "Something horrible could happen to them and I'd never recover." It took seconds to go from a flood of gratitude to a flash of terror. It is as if a dose of worry somehow keeps her safe and thinking about the worst case scenario somehow protects her from it.

I know how that goes. I lived that way for almost thirty years. If things were too good, too happy, and I was feeling too free…the next thing I knew, it was Red Alert! Danger, danger! The fort is not held down, the guard's asleep! Quick, find something to worry about. FAST, before all hell breaks loose.

I used to manufacture worry because I believed it kept me safe. I oh so mistakenly believed that worry was how I controlled my environment. I wouldn't be crushed when everything fell apart because I had predicted it. Anticipating and looking for what could go wrong was helping keep those awful things at bay. At the very least, I was becoming used to the idea of something bad happening so that nothing could shock me.

Maybe that's right.

But what if…the time spent feeling truly happy, enjoying our blessings, and staring lovingly, actually makes the uncertainty easier? What if we had it backwards?

What if something bad happened and you thought, "Some things ended, some things changed, but at least I was really, truly happy for a while." What if that thought actually makes the changes more manageable?

What if those moments of joy hold you up in your down times, instead of making the down times harder?

To test this crazy theory, maybe we could decide to be okay with not worrying, just as a trial run. Let yourself off the hook. Let yourself be happy. When you find yourself manufacturing worry, take a deep breath and stop. Release it.

Kindly remind yourself that worry doesn't help. But presence, appreciation, and love just might.

36

Fight for Your Right to Party

When I talk to people with chronic and habitual fear and worry they seem to want to look for ways to keep fear around.

"Doesn't fear have a purpose?"

Yes, fear serves a purpose at times. Real fear tells your body to prepare to fight or flee. But most of the time, our fear is not real. It's imagined.

"Isn't worry helpful, to some extent?" they ask, fighting for their right to worry. "Isn't it protective?"

Do you think you need protection from the fear that your mind invented in the first place? When it's useful fear, it prepares you for action. If you are sitting on your couch thinking about your fear, there is no upside. You are worrying to protect yourself from a threat that does not exist.

By and large in life, you are safe. You are protected. There's usually no actual danger in your path. Most likely, the dangerous outcome you are running from is a figment of your imagination. It's a byproduct of you being so damn smart and so damn creative and caring about your survival so much.

Your mind is the source of the false fear to begin with. To justify its actions, the mind throws a bunch of energy into protecting you from those fake threats.

Stop the cycle.

Know that you are totally safe, right now. If it doesn't feel like true knowing in the beginning, pretend that you are totally safe until you start to believe it.

From that place of safety, go one better. Devote the mental energy you used to spend worrying on creating something good.

Think about it this way: you wouldn't put "Breathe Air" on your to-do list. It's a given. So stop putting "Protect Self" there. When you take "Breathe Air" and "Protect Self" off your list, you make room for bigger, more creative, more fun ideas or activities. When you understand that you are safe and the threats to your well-being are false, you make room for better concerns.

Concerns like red or white. Or what you want to wear to the party this weekend. Or how you want to spend your year or how you want to spend your life. Fun stuff like that.

Assuming that you are safe saves a lot of time and energy that you get to use however you choose.

When you start using your energy the way you choose, your mind has less time to construct false threats for you to protect yourself against.

Party time.

37

When Fear is Good

If you want to be happier and more Enlightened, consider scaring yourself once and a while. We've all heard Eleanor Roosevelt's famous advice, "Do one thing every day that scares you."

Why is this important? I like doing what feels good, don't you? I'd rather spend my time throwing out the 'I-should' and 'I-have-to' stories and practicing extreme self-kindness.

So why would I recommend that you intentionally experience the ickiness of fear?

Because post-icky comes pure joy.

Research shows that we're happiest when we experience ourselves growing and evolving, becoming a greater, fuller version of who we are. Growth comes from feeling the fear and acting anyway.

Growth (and happiness) comes from playing to your edge. They come from straddling the very thick line between being so completely comfortable that we're numb or bored or asleep and being scared out of our gourd. There's a sweet spot in the middle and that sweet spot is absolute exhilaration.

Experiment a little and find your sweet spot. Think of something you want that sounds almost too scary to even say out loud, but is exhilarating at the same time. Then plan to do it.

When you step up the plate, know that the fear is going to be there waiting for you. It always is. Say, "Hello, fear; fancy meeting you here. I see you, and I'm going to go ahead and do this scary thing anyway." Then do the scary thing, feel the ickiness of fear, and experience the post-icky joy.

The joy, by the way, has nothing to do with succeeding at that scary thing. It's not about showing yourself that you can rock at something you thought you'd fail at. Sometimes—many times—you do fail at it. Become okay with that.

The joy comes from acting through the fear, regardless of the outcome.

38

Stuck, Stuck, Stuck

I can't tell you how many people each week tell me they're stuck. It's probably the most common thing I hear from my clients.

Although I know it's annoying, I first clarify that although they might feel stuck, they are not actually stuck. Unless you sat on spilled super glue or stepped into quicksand, you are not really stuck.

Everything is always in motion. "Progress" is always being made, most especially when we're resting or cocooning or doing something that doesn't look the way we expect progress to look. We are just really bad at evaluating what progress is and what it isn't. We often equate progress with movement, but there is progress in staying still, too. Like if you just went through a nasty break-up and you still can't get out of bed two weeks later, does that mean you aren't making progress? Nearly anyone living through this situation says yes, there is no progress there.

I totally disagree. You just lived through the first two weeks. Who cares if you didn't get out of bed, you got through the hardest part and it has to start getting easier eventually. You made a ton of progress lying in bed.

Most people think they are stuck because of their own self-inflicted standards for progress. Although resting and cocooning don't mean you're actually stuck, they feel like being stuck. That's because ninety-nine percent of feeling stuck is due to inaction. Take No Action equals Feel Stuck. Shocking, I know.

Action is scary as hell when you think you are stuck because you put so much pressure on doing something. You believe in the existence of things like "the right move" and "mistakes" and "messing up" and "the perfect choice."

But they don't exist, silly.

Have you noticed what it's like to take action when you don't feel stuck? When everything is going your way and life is flowing along like it's supposed to, you just ACT. You do something, without all the pressure and forethought. Those things usually turn out just fine. (They work out so fine that they actually reinforce your belief in a "right choice," but that's another story…)

So, remember two things:

Unless you can't physically move, you are not really stuck. You are just telling yourself you are and that's never a good story to choose.

And if you want to feel less stuck, move. Do something. Nothing reckless or irreversible, just make a normal-sized move. Repeat until you stop feeling stuck.

Part III

Surrender. Accept. Allow.

"Pain is simply the difference between what is and what I want it to be."
—Spencer Johnson

Surrender is accepting reality.

Surrender is *not* giving up, backing down, or quitting.

Surrender is the opposite of giving up. It's accepting what is so that you can move forward.

It's the place from which you must stand in order to progress. Accepting reality is the starting point for all good things.

It also happens to be the fastest path to the experience of freedom. When you argue with reality and *push against* what is, you experience pain and frustration. When you let go of that fight, the pain goes away.

This section is about all things surrender. From letting go of trying to control everything, to wanting what you want without *needing* it, to forgiveness. They all revolve around surrender and acceptance and they all make life much, much easier.

39

Let Go of Control:
Learning the Art of Surrender

"If we are facing in the right direction, all we have to do is keep on walking."

—Buddhist Proverb

I've noticed that things go much more smoothly when I give up control—when I allow them to happen instead of making them happen. Unfortunately, I'm terrible at this.

Although I'm much better than I used to be, I'm still a bit of a control freak. I often use perfectly good energy trying to plan, predict, and prevent things that I cannot possibly plan, predict, or prevent.

For example, I often wonder if my baby is going to get a proper nap when we travel and, if not, just how crabby she might be. I think through her travel and napping patterns attempting to figure out exactly what we're up against, as if her sleep is something I can control. I also over-plan for out-of-town guests. I spend my already-limited time planning for every possible weather/mood combination when considering our itinerary.

Like most humans I know, I spend a lot of time in business that's not mine: The baby's business, my friends' business, Mother Nature's business.

As a recovering control freak, there are three things I know for sure about trying to control things:

1. We try to control things because of what we think will happen if we don't.

In other words, control is rooted in fear.

2. Control is also a result of being attached to a specific outcome—an outcome we're sure is best for us, as if we always know what's best. When we trust that we're okay no matter what circumstances come our way, we don't need to micro-manage the universe. We let go. And we open ourselves to all sorts of wonderful possibilities that aren't there when we're attached to one "right" path.

3. The energy of surrender accomplishes much more than the energy of control.

I suspect it's slightly different for everyone, but here's what 'control mode' looks and feels like for me: My vision gets very narrow and focused, my breath is shallow, the adrenaline is pumping, and my heart rate increases. My mind shifts from topic to topic, from past to future very quickly, and I have little concentration, poor memory, and almost no present-moment awareness.

In surrender mode, I'm calm, peaceful, breathing deeply, and present in the moment. I see clearly and my vision extends out around me, allowing me to (literally) see the bigger picture. The great irony is that by attempting to control things I actually feel less in control. When I'm micro-managing and obsessing over details, I know I'm getting in my own way.

The Art of Surrender

Surrender literally means to stop fighting. Stop fighting with yourself, stop fighting the universe and the natural flow of things and stop resisting and pushing against reality.

Surrender equals Complete Acceptance of what is plus Faith that all is well, even without my input. Surrender isn't inaction. It's about taking action when you are feeling the calm energy of surrender.

If letting go of control and surrendering not only feels better, but actually produces better results, sign me up, right? But wait….how do we surrender? Sometimes it's as easy as noticing that you are in control mode and choosing to let go—by consciously and deliberately shifting into surrender energy.

For example, when I become aware that I'm in control mode, I imagine that I'm in a small canoe paddling upstream, against the current. It's hard. It's a fight. That's what control mode feels like to me. When I choose to let go and surrender, I visualize turning the boat around, dropping the oars, and floating downstream. I'm being gently pulled, no effort necessary on my part. Simply breathing and saying, "Let go of the oars," is usually enough to get me there.

Sometimes it's a little harder to make the shift from control to surrender. Here are a few questions to ask yourself that can help:

1. What am I afraid will happen if I let go of control?

When you pinpoint the fear, question its validity. If you are afraid the night will be ruined if your boyfriend doesn't remember to pick up eggplant for dinner (and you've already reminded him fourteen times), question your assumption. Can you really know the night would be ruined without the eggplant? And if it would be ruined (by your definition, anyway), what's so bad about that?

2. Find out whose business you are in.

Your business is the realm of things that you can directly influence. Are you there? Or are you in someone else's business? When we're trying to control things outside of our own business, it's not going to go well.

3. Consider this: Would letting go feel like freedom?

It almost always would. Let that feeling of freedom guide you toward loosening your grip.

A Friendly Universe

Albert Einstein said, "The most important decision we make is whether we believe we live in a friendly or hostile universe."

I believe in a friendly universe.

Being receptive and allowing things to happen is a skill that can be practiced and improved upon. It helps to believe in a friendly universe— one that is supporting you at every turn so that you don't have to worry yourself over the details.

There is a peaceful, yet focused energy that accompanies holding the intention of what I want, but not forcing myself to do it. That energy is magic. I'm still a work in progress, but I'm allowing it to become a habit instead of making it a habit.

We can always choose to do things the easy way or the hard way. We can muscle through, or we can let go of the oars and let the current carry us downstream.

40

All Anxiety is
Caused by Just One Thing

I'm beginning to think all anxiety in life comes from our attempt to control things.

Anxiety and I are pretty tight. I've been on all sides: coaching tons of people through it, coaching myself through it, and before all that, being nearly debilitated because of it.

My decades of "research" into anxiety are pointing to one single underlying cause: control. That's what I think it all boils down to.

Think about the things you think cause your anxiety. Make a quick list.

Your list probably includes things like money, time pressure, fearful thinking, too much coffee, or too much stress.

I agree that all of these things trigger anxiety. But there's something else going on.

Your thoughts go much deeper than these surface issues. Your thoughts are most likely arguing with reality.

Anytime you think things should be different or need to be different or it would be really, really nice if they were different than they are, you are attempting to control reality. And that, in my opinion, is what causes all anxiety. Thinking about the past doesn't automatically cause anxiety... unless we're wishing things had been different.

Thinking about the future doesn't create anxiety...unless we're mentally playing out how it has to look. And thinking about the present... well, you get the idea.

When we surrender and let go of our need to control, anxiety lets go of us. Just like that.

41

Non-Attachment?
Or Simply Not Choosing?

I have a client who used to live his life in the future. He was always in his head, planning, predicting, and trying to figure things out before they occurred. It wasn't all that pleasant for him, as you can imagine. So, he started working through that and he made some shifts—except he shifted a little too much.

Rather than trying to figure everything out and stay ten steps ahead of the game, he adopted a laid-back, "What's meant to happen will happen," approach which involved him no longer making any choices.

In fact, he didn't think much at all about what he wanted. He was basically reacting rather than creating, in the name of, "Que sera, sera. I'm just taking life as it comes." He called it non-attachment, when it's actually anything but. Non-attachment doesn't mean not choosing. It means choosing, but knowing that you'll be okay no matter what you get.

You still set your intentions, place your order, and go for what you want. The non-attachment part refers to the fact that your happiness is not attached to those dreams coming true in the exact way you expect them to. What he was doing was more like resigning.

Ironically, what he called non-attachment was just the opposite. It was extreme attachment. He was very attached to not experiencing the frustration, disappointment, or embarrassment he thought he would experience if he said he wanted something and then didn't get it. He was so attached to avoiding those unpleasant emotions that he began reacting rather than creating so he could pretend he didn't care.

Non-attachment is a mindset, not a behavior. If fact, if it looks like anything, it probably looks like choosing more. When you know you are okay anyway, you feel free to dream all kinds of big dreams.

So, place your order. Make it big, and see it as clearly as you can. Then practice non-attachment by having faith that you always get what's for your greatest good, even when it doesn't look that way at first. Know that you will be okay, and all is well, no matter what specific outcomes roll your way.

42

Responsibility versus Blame

Do you know the difference between responsibility and blame?

Responsibility is empowering. It's powerful. It's all good. When you take responsibility for your life, you put yourself in the driver's seat. When you take responsibility for having hurt someone, you accept what you did so that you can learn from your mistakes and move on. Responsibility equals Acceptance. No wonder it feels so good to finally take responsibility after having shirked it.

Blame, on the other hand, is disempowering. When you blame yourself for the state of your life, you are living in the past. When you blame yourself for having hurt someone else, you experience shame and shame has no upside.

When you take responsibility for having hurt someone else you may wish things had been different, but you ultimately accept reality. That's responsibility. Responsibility has a huge upside. It's motivating and liberating. You can create from a place of having taken responsibility.

Blame? No upside. It only makes you feel bad which leaves you unmotivated and imprisoned. You are left to react from a place of blame.

So, if you are blaming yourself or another person or some circumstance for the state of your life, you are standing in your own way.

Instead, take responsibility for every single thing in your life (AND everything you believe is missing from it). This means the wanted and unwanted stuff. All of it.

When you accept it as it is you are now free to create something new.

43

You are Doing Exactly
What You Want to Do

I hear a lot of people say that they want to do things that they are not doing. I say they don't really want to do those things. They only think they want to.

You might say, "I really want to write a book," or "I'd love to be a long-distance runner," but if you don't write and you don't run, you don't really want to do what you *say* you want to do. I hear all the arguments. You really do want to write, you just don't have the time, or you are too tired, or you don't have the right materials. Or you really do want to run, you just don't know where to start, or you are scared, or you are not cleared by your doctor.

I would say that if you really and truly want to write or run, you do it. You would find a way and go for it without much effort. It's not hard. It's just what you do. It's like when you get up with a crying baby in the middle of the night. You are exhausted and there are many excuses to not to get up, but you don't even bother generating excuses. Your legs start walking toward the baby's room with or without your consent.

So if you are not doing a particular thing, you may *think* you want to, but you probably don't really want to. If you are standing in front of the refrigerator and you have to ask, "Am I hungry?" you are not. If you were hungry you'd eat. It's when you are only thinking about being hungry, that you ask.

See the difference? Writing and running—same thing.

To look at the other side of the coin, it's also true that whatever you are doing right now, you want to be doing. That's a tough one, I know. I have clients who swear up and down that they don't want to be in the job or the city or the financial situation they're in. They sing in the church choir and they say they hate the church choir.

But if you don't want to be doing it, why are you? No one's holding a gun to your head. There are consequences to every choice we make and those consequences complicate things. We say we want a better financial situation, but the truth of the matter is that we don't want to work the crappy job *more than* we want money. We say we want to quit the church choir but the truth is we want to feel needed *more than* we want to quit.

I get it. Sometimes it's not fair and we really want two things that are conflicting and we can't get them both. But make no mistake—you are always choosing the one you want more. When money becomes more important than working a crappy job, you'll have money. When running becomes more important than being nervous or uninformed, you'll be a runner.

There are no right or wrong choices here, either. I'd totally rather be a non-runner and (many days) a non-writer. The reason I know that is because I am. Although I think I'd like to run and write, it's crystal clear to me that I don't really want to all that much because I'm not.

The reason for pointing this out is just so that you know for sure—you are choosing the life you have. That means you can always (always, always, always) choose differently.

When you really want to, that is.

44

Truth or La, La, La

We were at dinner the other night with our friends (another couple) and their teenage daughter.

Our friends had just returned from a vacation and they had left both teenage daughters at home. I asked the one who was having dinner with us, "So did you and your sister throw some wild parties while your parents were gone?" As soon as I asked the question, her dad covered his ears and said, "La, la, la," to avoid hearing the truth.

Which got me thinking about how much I "La, la, la," in my own life when I don't want to know the truth about something. Truth is king. Truth allows you to practice acceptance which you probably know is the cornerstone of all harmony. Accepting the truth allows you to move forward. Truth sets you free. Truth—even when it's unwanted—has an undercurrent of peace.

But I've been accused on many occasions of being an advocate of "La, la, la."

I won't watch the news or listen to people talk about dogs or babies dying. I have no clue what the murder statistics are in Chicago, although some of that stuff is happening in my own backyard.

What I've realized about this is that if it's something I can't or am not willing to do something about, I'd rather "La, la, la." Sure, the honorable choice might be to educate myself on the murder stats and volunteer to help the cause, but I'm not being led toward that. Thank God other people are inspired to do that work because I'm really not. So if it's not going to help me feel peace and/or move forward in life, I'd rather not have my energy drained by the miserable details.

I'm guessing that's exactly why my friend "La, la, la-ed" rather than listened to the truth about his daughters' parties. Their girls are seventeen and eighteen, super sweet, responsible, and respectful. Because the girls and the home were unharmed when he returned from vacation, knowing whether or not they had a party wouldn't serve him in any positive way.

You have to figure out what you need to know and what you don't. There's always a trade off.

Many times, knowing the truth will be worth the trouble it might cause. But sometimes knowing the whole truth just makes you feel crappy and the pay-offs are not worth it. Hearing sad stories or crime statistics when there is nothing I can or intend to do to change things only causes unnecessary pain.

45

Affirm and Add

One of the tools we used in my training to become a master life coach was improvisational comedy. The word "improv" incites sheer panic for a control freak like me.

I'm going to stand in front of these people whose approval I cared way too much about and try to be funny on the spot? No preparation, no thinking about it, no research, or no planning? Just being.... natural? Yeah, right.

The first rule of improv comedy is Affirm and Add. When someone says, "Look, a bear!" you Affirm: "Yes!" and Add: "And he's reading the Old Testament while sitting on the toilet!" There's no negating: "That's not a bear, that's my wife!" Or even, "A bear? Where?" which is a weaker form of negating. The rule is to Affirm like it's the best idea you've ever heard, and then expand on it.

Sound simple? It's not.

This rule sounded so easy to me that I didn't give it a second thought. I was busy mentally rehearsing the other rules of improv, figuring that rule number one would be a natural. It was all good, until I got into my scene (in which I was one of three amnesiacs at an airport) and found myself wanting to negate everything. What's so hard about accepting what someone else throws at you? What's with this very natural tendency—I'd even go as far as calling it a default automatic response—to fight against what we're given?

In improv and in life, sometimes we fight against What Is because we have another idea in mind and we don't want to change it. Sometimes we fight against What Is because we go blank in the moment and we're used to saying no more often than we are to saying yes. Sometimes we just want to control the scene.

It's true in improv and true in life.

Remember, how you do anything is how you do everything. Improv showed me our natural tendency to negate, fight against, argue, and resist. Which is too bad, because we all know the Enlightened path is to accept, accept, accept, and accept. When we accept exactly where we are and expand from there, we are light years ahead of where we are when we resist and try to change.

Think "Yes, AND", not "No, BUT".

You lost your job. "Yes, AND I'm going to find a new one," is actually so much easier than saying "No! BUT I will starve to death and end up homeless without that job!" When you are recognizing painful patterns that have held you back in life, saying, "Yes AND that is wonderful because now I'm aware" is so much easier than, "No! BUT if I didn't have these damn patterns I'd be happy and successful by now."

Yes, AND. Affirm and Add. Accept and expand from there.

46

Why I Told the Truth

I experienced something really, really cool one weekend—how to release the pressure and watch your painful story disintegrate before your eyes. How do you release the pressure? Tell the Truth.

Hubby, baby, and I had just returned from a typical summer Saturday afternoon: checked out a Chicago street festival, had lunch, pushed baby on the swing at the park, and stopped at Target on the way home. I love days like this. We had been home for about an hour. Baby was hyper, crawling all over me and hubby on the couch. Hubby watched the baby with one eye and the TV with the other. I watched the baby with one eye and started feeling BORED.

I'm sitting with my family, I just had a fun afternoon and it's not like we'd been sitting there all day. I have the most adorable baby in the world who I really, really wanted and went through hell to have. And I'm bored. I want the baby to go to sleep so I can leave, or go do something. Or I want to write, or read a book, or work on my website, or clean something. All things I can't do with a hyper baby and the baby is not about to go to sleep.

I'm not happy and that's so, so wrong. The mental dialogue starts. You know, the one where you judge yourself for feeling the way you feel:

I'm not the mom-type.

I have no patience.

What's wrong with me that I'd rather read a book than play with my baby?

My husband is a frickin' saint.

He's so patient, so content, so in the moment, and so much better than me.

Way better than me.

No wonder the baby loves him more.

I'm so selfish.

I'm a terrible mother.

There is a right and a wrong way to be happy and I am wrong.

None of these thoughts were new, which only made them feel more true.

But…the way I handled them that day was brand new. Instead of noticing them and letting them pitch a tent in my mind, and instead of instantly diving in and trying to coach myself through them, I released them.

I let them out.

I told hubby exactly what I was thinking. I cried. I told him how I had expected motherhood to change me, how I thought I'd want to spend every second watching her and that reading or writing or any of the things I used to love would suddenly pale in comparison. I explained how something was clearly wrong with me, because that didn't happen. I still enjoyed solitary activities and silence. I told him how I wanted her to sleep so that I could do my own selfish things again.

He laughed the nicest laugh I've ever heard and explained that I was crazy, but not in the straight-jacket kind of way I was thinking. I won't go into it all (but he really is a frickin' saint).

The important part is, a really, really cool and interesting thing happened. I felt so much better after I let out my truth, but that's not all.

The interesting thing is that for the rest of that day, and for all of the next day, I really did want to chase my little girl around the house and listen to her babble. My husband took a break from the baby and raved about how patient I was. He offered me a break and I turned it down. Seriously, I didn't even want it.

When I Told the Truth, I released the pressure. My story went away. By saying it out loud I freed it from the prison of my mind. I didn't experience the boredom any more. My resistance to it was making it so much more real than it really was.

And the shame wasn't there. Well, not as much.

I know the boredom will come back some day, but that's okay now. Boredom is fine; I can do boredom. It is boredom and a story about how it makes me a terrible person that really stinks.

47

Moving Forward by Walking Away

At one time in my life I moved a lot. Without fail, a couple weeks before my moving date I'd meet a great guy who was firmly planted in the city I was moving away from. Or, I'd meet some fun new friends, or discover a hidden gem of a restaurant I never knew about while I lived there. It always happened right before I left.

When there were only a few weeks left at my summer job, the job suddenly got really interesting. When I finally decided to end things with the boyfriend du jour, he'd do something super nice out of the blue and turn into the guy I always wanted him to be. Something would always come up in the eleventh hour to make me fall back in love with what I was about to walk away from.

Have you ever experienced this? I don't know why this happens but I have a theory…

Take the boyfriend. Putting myself back in that time, I can remember the feeling of relief that came from deciding to dump him. I was no longer responsible for scolding or changing him; what would be the point? I could finally let him be himself, knowing our time together was coming to an end.

Clearly, letting him be who he was had everything to do with him becoming kinder toward me. That's my leading theory: When we are about to walk away we stop trying to change everything. We let things be the way they naturally are, because our involvement is essentially over.

When we let things be the way they naturally are, magic happens. We drop the struggle. We accept What Is instead of fighting against it, because what's the use of fighting?

When we think we might grow old in a particular city or in a career or with a particular dude, there's a lot at stake. We're in it. We like some things and we dislike others but if we're in it, we want the things we dislike to change—fast.

So we control, grasp, fight, and resist What Is, and we get locked in place. We're stuck. Imagine two people pushing against each other as hard as they can. They don't move because the forces cancel each other out and they're both immobilized. When one drops his arms, the other goes flying forward. The more pressure they were putting out, the further and harder they fall.

When we let go, we finally move. Deciding to walk away from your city or job or man just makes it easier to let go because it's not personal anymore. Walking away makes room for what you always wanted but you don't have to walk away to let go. You can practice letting go, little by little, while you are still in it.

You can do this by letting the guy be who he is, dropping your agenda for him, and loving him now. You can do this by appreciating where you live and all it has to offer, and acting every day as if you were moving tomorrow.

You can do this by working your tail off at the job, taking the time to get to know your coworkers, and investing the extra time in that project instead of railing against it because there's no end in sight.

That's how you get to move forward even when you are not walking away.

48

Surrender and Release in Action (or How I Got Over my First Love)

After four years together, my first love and I broke up during our freshman year of college. It was mutual and somewhat expected. I took it surprisingly well at first.

Until—just a few weeks after our break-up—I found out he was already dating someone else. It was someone we both knew and someone he had been friends with throughout our relationship. I suspected she always had a thing for him. That's when I lost it. And, I did devastation good, like the loss of a first love should be. I didn't get out of bed for over a week. I missed classes, appointments, and exams. Because it was too much effort to talk to anyone, I didn't bother letting my professors know what was going on. I destroyed the 4.0 GPA I had up to that point.

I didn't eat anything for four days. My roommates snuck bagels from the cafeteria into my top bunk but I wouldn't touch them. I finally drank some Gatorade after they threatened to call my mom.

One day, from half under the covers in my top bunk, I caught a glimpse of a book my mom had tucked away in my suitcase. It was called *A Return to Love* by Marianne Williamson. It was based on another book called *A Course in Miracles*.

I sure as hell needed a miracle.

Flipping to the section called Relationships, I read things like:

There are only two emotions: love and fear.

If I project guilt onto another person, I always end up feeling more guilty.

Pain doesn't stem from the love we're denied by others, but rather from the love we deny them.

I didn't understand it completely the time, but I was intrigued. The book shifted my attention away from my pain for the first time in a week. The book explained that although it feels like we're hurt by what someone did to us, what really hurts is that their closed heart tempted us to close our own. It's our own denial of love that hurts us.

As a way to end the judgment and re-open our own hearts, forgiveness is the key. Specifically, Marianne Williamson told how she got over heartbreak by forgiving her ex and releasing him to the Holy Spirit. She repeated the mantra "I forgive Mike and release him to the Holy Spirit." I was supposed to do the same with my ex.

Forgiveness would change my perception. Releasing him to the Holy Spirit meant handing my pain over to something bigger that could heal it for me, since I clearly wasn't doing a very good job on my own. I repeated the mantra until I fell back asleep. The next day, I got out of bed and said it some more. I walked all over campus reciting that mantra again and again and again in my mind: "I forgive him and release him to the Holy Spirit. I forgive him and release him to the Holy Spirit."

I did this for days on end. At some point, I forgave the girl he was dating and released her, too. Then I forgave myself—for being weak, for not keeping it together, for ever imagining our wedding, for letting myself be vulnerable, for wrecking my GPA—and I released myself, too. With every step across campus, I forgave. With the next step, I released. I forgave, I released.

Finally I felt better. Not just better, but saved. I was over it and somehow lifted up. It certainly felt like a miracle.

Fast Forward

Fast forward twelve years. I was working with an incredible coach who was helping me through the grief I felt over not being able to get pregnant. She taught me to surrender and release any lingering thoughts or emotions I didn't want.

"I'll never get pregnant," was to become, "I surrender and release the fear that I'll never get pregnant."

The fleeting, "It's not fair," that loitered in my mind became, "I surrender and release the thought that it's not fair."

Just like forgiving and releasing my ex-boyfriend, I could surrender to and release any unwanted thought or emotion. Maybe not instantly, but the practice of monitoring my thoughts long enough to surrender and release them helped me feel in control again.

There was something clear and concrete I could do (notice the thoughts, surrender to them) to help myself heal. There was a lot I didn't have to do, because I was releasing them to something bigger in order to heal.

Now I forgive and release and surrender and release all the time. If there's someone I need to forgive, or something I'm better off surrendering to, I know the words that feel like magic. And I still always get my miracle.

49

Let it Go, Already

Many people seem to think that forgiveness has something to do with the "bad guy" who did something wrong. I've heard people say they won't forgive for all kinds of reasons:

- The bad guy doesn't deserve forgiveness.
- He doesn't see the error in his ways.
- He did the bad thing intentionally.
- It's unforgiveable.

As if any of those have anything at all to do with forgiveness.

Forgiveness is a gift you give yourself. It has absolutely nothing to do with anyone else. Think about it. If you are upset over what someone else did and you are living with your anger at them, who are you hurting? You are certainly not hurting them. They probably have no idea you are angry and even if they do, they probably don't care. They're probably out drinking a margarita right now, dancing in the club, laughing at a joke, and not thinking about you at all. They're going on with their life while you are living with negative emotion. How could your act of forgiveness have anything at all to do with them?

Forgive them and quit hurting yourself.

I did a radio spot the other day about relationships. The interviewer asked me, "What's a reasonable amount of time to hold a grudge?" I said, "Well, how long do you want to feel like crap?" Grudges don't teach lessons. And it's not your job to teach anyone else a lesson, anyway. Grudges only ensure that you keep generating anger and you are the one who is experiencing that anger.

You may think that forgiving someone lets them off the hook, but the person it really lets off the hook is you. You get to let go of the anger so that it no longer runs its destructive course through your body. You win emotional freedom. So why don't we just let it go, already? Why does it feel so hard? I think it's the belief that holding on to anger protects us from future transgressions. We think if we forgive, we condone what was done, and that somehow leaves us vulnerable to more of the same treatment.

The exact opposite is true. When we forgive and truly release it, we show the Universe that this bad thing that was done to us isn't part of who we are. It's irrelevant. It has no power over us anymore. We stop believing that things should have been different than they were. We accept what was so that we can move forward.

Forgiveness of another person requires forgiveness of ourselves, too. Holding on to anger keeps us feeling right, and it keeps them in the wrong. Except that doesn't feel much better, does it?

We can let it all go. Forgive the bad guy, forgive ourselves for letting him hurt us, and let it go already. It's time.

50

Releasing versus Avoiding

My client Patty is afraid of conflict. She usually runs away and avoids speaking up in the hopes that her problems go away on their own.

She doesn't call it running away though. She calls it turning the other cheek. She tells me she's being Enlightened.

I correct her. "Don't lie to yourself, Patty," I say. "It's running. It's far from Enlightened."

She asks: Aren't there times when simply walking away is the Enlightened thing to do? Isn't that called "taking the high road"? What's the difference between ignoring something in an Enlightened way versus ignoring it because I'm hiding? These are excellent questions.

"Ignoring" something in an Enlightened way is called Letting It Go. You are releasing it. You are no longer holding onto it by paying attention to it. You know it when you do it because it feels good. It literally feels like a release in your body. You feel lighter. Not weighed down with the extra burden.

Ignoring something because you don't want to face it is not Letting It Go, it's Avoidance.

Avoidance feels heavy, not light. You are still weighed down by the issue because avoidance doesn't make things go away, it makes them grow. The issue will follow you around. You'll get an ulcer or migraines or have nightmares about it. Random things will pop up to remind you of the issue you are trying to avoid. The problem gets worse, not better.

If you are unsure if your personal flavor of ignoring is Letting It Go or Avoidance, just wait and watch the "problem." Pay attention to how you feel. It will become very clear, very soon.

Part IV

In Relationship with Yourself

"It's your relationship with yourself that determines the quality of virtually every experience that comes your way."

—Sandra Anne Taylor

Nearly everyone I know holds themselves to some pretty high standards. Sometimes we inherited those standards. Many times, we invented them and placed them on ourselves.

Life would be so much easier if we could all decide that we're doing just fine in life regardless of how we "measure up." Can we?

Can you?

Can you deem yourself "good enough" just by virtue of being alive? Can you somehow find a way to love and appreciate yourself the way you love and appreciate others?

Could you speak to yourself the way you'd speak to an innocent child? Or, shower yourself with the respect you wish other people showed you?

Can you let yourself off the hook for not being perfect? Or better yet, love yourself more for your imperfections?

Well, if you can, you seriously rock. You are way ahead of the curve.

If you are not quite there but you are willing to work on it, this section is for you.

51

Self-Love: A Letter to My Daughter

I asked my husband the other day what he thinks is most important for our daughter to learn. If he could have her learn just one life lesson, what would it be?

He said to be kind to others.

That sounds nice and I understand where he's coming from. But as someone who coaches women who are dissatisfied and out of touch with what they want, that idea makes me nervous. As a perfectionist and one time "approval whore," it terrifies me.

I'd rather she learn to be kind to herself.

Little girls all over the world are raised to be nice. We are taught to go out of our way to do things for others, often at the expense of our own desires. If our desires appear too self-centered, they're considered wrong and aren't validated. But, how could our desires not be self-centered? They're our desires. They're supposed to center on ourselves, that's why they're ours.

I've seen far too many grown women stare blankly when asked, "What do you want?" or "What would make you happy right now?" They forget that wanting what they want is even an option. Over a lifetime, they eventually lose touch with their own longings and forget who they really are. I believe there's nothing more natural and important than being self-centered. Not to the detriment of others, but in a way that means we make it our primary duty in life to discover and practice what makes us happy. We fill our own cup first.

All of this nice girl stuff is based on one huge lie, anyway: that something outside of us can make us happy. We walk around pretending that we have the ability to make others feel good and if we're really lucky, they'll make us feel good in return. Doesn't it make more sense for us to all take responsibility for our own happiness? That way we could enjoy other people for who they are without trying to manipulate and change them.

When you realize that others are responsible for their own happiness, you stop trying so hard to be the source of their joy. You let them do that job themselves, because they're the only ones who can. Then you can turn your focus to finding your own joy, because you are the only one who can.

If we all made our own happiness our number one priority, the world would be completely different. There would be no scarcity mentality— we'd realize nothing is really in short supply because everything we ever need is inside us, always.

Not needing others (but still wanting them) leads to much more kindness.

Not relying on others to make us happy takes a lot of pressure off.

With permission to focus on our own positive feelings, we'd naturally realize that being kind feels good. It feels even better when we do it with no agenda. We'd go from trying to control someone else's happiness to practicing kindness for our own selfish reasons.

Doesn't that sound *nice*?

52

Self-Esteem Isn't
All it's Cracked Up to Be

Holding yourself in high esteem seems really important, doesn't it?
It's nice to think positive thoughts about yourself and that's exactly what self-esteem is: making favorable evaluative judgments about good ol' you. Self-esteem comes from the thoughts and beliefs you have about yourself. And, as you know, thoughts and beliefs are not objective, observable facts; they're subjective judgments and personal interpretations.

As I'm sure you can guess, this is going to get messy—fast. In order to evaluate yourself, you need some standards (i.e., beliefs) you subscribe to, right? You'll need to invent those standards—or borrow them from somewhere else—in order to judge yourself. Otherwise, how would you know which evaluation to make?

So you invent some definitions to use to decide whether you are "good" or "bad." Or you pick up some from your parents, the neighbor kid, your church, or the president and you use those to decide whether you are good or bad. Maybe you decide that if you are nice, smart, brunette, not too wealthy, and straight, you'll judge yourself as good. If you are loud, opinionated, rich, mean, or a minority, you are you are bad.

Then you tally it all up. Not consciously or explicitly, but you are always keeping a tally. Are there mostly good judgments? Congratulations! You have high self-esteem. Are there more bad than good? You have low self-esteem.

Of course, part of what really sets you up for trouble is standards that are beyond your control. If you decide your self-esteem is based on how well you do at your job or how good a friend you are, eventually you are going to mess up at work or fight with your friend and you'll be cornered into judging yourself poorly. Your self-esteem will plummet until you go out and make a new friend or garner some praise from the corner office.

Before you know it, you are stuck in a cycle where the way you feel about yourself is based on outside circumstances. As those circumstances fluctuate, the way you view yourself dips and soars like a roller coaster.

Self-esteem isn't sounding so great anymore, is it?

The Alternative to Self-Esteem

The alternative to self-esteem is self-acceptance.

Self-acceptance is just what it sounds like: accepting yourself, period. There are no evaluations involved. You don't have to invent standards and then judge yourself based on them. You simply decide to accept yourself regardless of what's going on around or within you.

Self-esteem is conditional; self-acceptance is unconditional. You are not chasing the carrot anymore. There is no more roller coaster.

Self-acceptance is much simpler than self-esteem. But is it easier? No way. Not at first, anyway.

We're programmed to think in terms of good and bad. We evaluate and judge everything. Self-acceptance requires a degree of separation from all of that along with the willingness to question your standards and let them go.

Self-acceptance requires letting go of the superficial, external circumstances of your life and making a decision to love yourself unconditionally, regardless.

If you don't know where to start and if waking up tomorrow and deciding to love yourself feels like too far of a stretch, start with willingness. Be willing to accept yourself no matter what without needing to actually do it right away.

Your willingness allows the barriers to crack and crumble. It will start to come together from there.

53

How to be Adorable

If you want to be adored—and let's face it, who doesn't?—be adorable. When you are adorable—when you love and adore yourself—it shows. It looks like radiant confidence. You look smoking hot. It is knowing without a doubt, that as soon as they get to know you, they'll love and adore you, too.

My baby can teach you how. We flew cross-country with her when she was six months old. There was no doubt in her mind that every person on that plane was in love with her. She worked the plane, standing on our laps and smiling at the stone-faced business travelers and the people wearing eye masks and headphones. She tilted her head and blew kisses as if they were her adoring fans. They soon were. She adored them. And she clearly adores herself. She won them over, big time.

Her dad and I had another story going. It went something like Oh-no-we're-"the people with the baby"-and-everyone-is-hoping-we-don't-sit-near-them. We didn't make eye contact with anyone while boarding because we imagined they were all avoiding eye contact with us. We weren't being very adorable. And I don't think we were very adored.

She's a year older now, and she made me think of this again last week. As we walked a few blocks down a crowded sidewalk, she was holding my hand and waving to every man, woman, and dog with her other hand.

"Hi-eee!" she yelled to everyone in earshot, waving frantically. She said, "Hi-eee dawdy," to all the dogs.

People waved back and said, "Hi-eee little girl!" Wives pinched their husband's arms and pointed to her, saying, "Look, how cute!" Dogs ran over to lick the hand she was holding out to them. Even cool teenagers hanging out with their friends cracked smiles. I saw them. She knew it would happen that way. There was never any doubt in her mind. She took the risk of reaching out to strangers because she doesn't know any better. But it wasn't really a risk at all. When you are adorable, you are adored.

Most of being adorable is taking the "risk" of putting yourself out there to others, and being willing to show your adorableness.

I'm learning this lesson from her. The next time I want more adoration, I'm going to try to be adorable first. It works for her so it could probably work for me. And for you, too.

54

Why You Don't Love
Yourself More. And How To.

We love ourselves just fine at first. Then something happens. I vividly remember this shift from my own childhood.

I would have an idea I just knew was outright brilliant. I couldn't wait to see the look of amazement on adult faces when I told them. Except when I revealed my idea, it was immediately shot down. Really? I was wrong about that?

Or I'd say something I just knew would make my adults roll on the floor in laughter. They'd think, "Damn, that girl of ours is hilarious!" Except when I delivered my punch-line I was told to stop goofing off. They didn't even crack a smile.

Of course as kids we don't consider that maybe our adults are simply grumpy or have no sense of humor or can't recognize our brilliance because of their own stuff. Kids always (always, always) assume they are the cause of everything. It's the way our brains develop. The world

153

revolves around us and we're the cause of everything. So 'kid-think' goes: if they didn't like my idea it's because I'm not smart enough. If they didn't laugh it's because I'm not funny. How could it be any other way?

And just like that, we don't love ourselves the same because beliefs are planted:

- I'm not as smart as I thought.
- I'm not as funny as I thought.
- I'm not quite good enough.
- It's in my best interest to find out what they want and be that. That's the only sure way to get the love and approval I need to survive.

After awhile, we're really in a pickle. We've spent so much time trying to figure out what they want that we're not quite sure what we want. We still want love and approval, we know that much. But when we're waiting for that approval from someone else, here's how it's going to turn out:

- We try to predict what they want from us and we deliver that.
- Their approval is inconsistent because it's not about us, it's about them. Sometimes they'll feel like approving, sometimes they won't, no matter what we do,
- Then, we're left more disillusioned than ever. We thought we were doing everything right. Now we not only don't have the kind of approval we're craving, but we're not even being the real us. We're not feeling the love, and the cycle continues.

There's really only one solution.

You have to be the generator of the love you've been waiting for. Any other source of that love and approval might feel nice but it's not sustainable. It's not something you can rely on or control or influence very much.

Clients tell me all the time that love and approval seems better—more valid, more deserved—when they come from someone else. The reason it feels that way is because you are still in that little kid mode of trusting others more than you trust yourself. Unfortunately, now you've trained yourself into that mode as an adult. You've stopped trusting your own judgment and respecting yourself. But I have good news for you: beginning to trust and respect your own judgment again is easier than it sounds.

You just start. Start small, but start.

1. Say, "I love that about me," often.

The more unsure you are, the more you should say it. I get mad at my husband for something that wasn't his fault. Again. I apologize to him and silently say to myself, "I did it again and I apologized. I love that about me." I'm wishing I was better than I am at something. I love that about me. I got caught in the rain and show up for the meeting soaking wet with mascara streaks down my face. I love that about me.

2. Practice seeing yourself the way you see some living thing you totally adore.

Babies and pets work well for this. There's your dog, so excited to see you, so adorable, loving, and cuddly. Transfer those feelings to yourself. Swooooosh…move it from over there on the dog to over here on you. Now *you* are excited, adorable, loving, and cuddly. The way you feel about the dog…feel that way about yourself.

3. Begin listening to yourself, first.

Don't look for advice so much. Don't ask other people what they think all the time. Don't even share what you are up to if you are doing so with an agenda of seeking approval. Just do what feels right to you and let that be enough. It's your business and your life, not theirs.

4. Notice how little you judge others.

Actually, you probably envy them for stepping out of the mold and being themselves, don't you? Why would different rules apply when it comes to you?

5. Remember that when you were a kid and your ideas and jokes fell flat all it means is that your parents weren't in the mood for a joke.

It was about them, not you.

You don't have to remember specific instances like I do, just know that unless you were raised by wolves, this happened to you, too. You had no choice then but to assume you weren't good enough, but now you do have a choice. It doesn't mean what your five year old brain made it mean.

Practice and repeat. Often.

Sound too simple? Try it for a while first, please. Thinking, "This is too simplistic; that will never work for me," is a cover-up for fear. I know change can feel scary. But you can handle a little fear—you've survived much worse.

55

One General Piece of Advice

In the movie *How Do You Know?* Reese Witherspoon's character asks her therapist: "Is there one general piece of advice that can help almost anyone in almost any situation?"

Good question.

What's your answer? You may not be a psychologist or a life coach and you may not help people find their way in any formal sense. But your words, advice, and example change lives. Probably much more than you even know.

So what is one general piece of advice you think can help almost anyone in almost any situation?

The therapist in the movie said: "Figure out what you want and learn how to ask for it."

I like that answer.

If I had to answer the question, I'd find it difficult. There are so many possibilities. But I think I'd have to go with: "Treat yourself the way you'd treat an innocent little child." Because at the root of almost every problem

I've ever seen with anyone is a failure to cut themselves some slack. There is failure to relax and failure to choose to love themselves right now, not once they meet some self-imposed condition.

What an interesting question though, don't you think?

56

Dealing with
I-Should-Be-Better Syndrome

"When you realize there is nothing lacking, the whole world belongs to you."

—Lao Tzu

Nearly everyone I know thinks they should be doing better in some way.

Are you totally and completely satisfied with what you've done so far in life? Isn't there a little part of you that thinks, maybe I should have more money in the bank? Or maybe I should have a more professional wardrobe, or a book contract, or a dog that's housebroken? The word "should" is not exactly enlightened or peaceful. Nor is the practice of judging yourself or believing that you are not exactly where you are meant to be. But we're human so our thoughts inevitably go to "should" from time to time.

We judge ourselves. We hold ourselves to standards that someone else made up—standards that may not even make sense for our current life.

We say things like:

"I can't believe I'm in my forties and still don't have matching luggage."

"Shouldn't my child be reading by now?"

"I always assumed I'd exercise regularly after I finished college."

"I can't believe I don't have a retirement fund."

I have to wonder, whose beliefs are those? Whose standards are they, really? It's not like we wake up at forty and suddenly crave matching luggage. Someone fed us that expectation somewhere along the way, and we forgot it wasn't our own.

Would a mother feel genuine concern for her child's reading skills if they lived on a deserted island? Or is the pressure external, based on what others say, think, and read, and she simply doesn't realize those thoughts aren't hers?

I, too, have thoughts like these all the time. Not these exactly, but ones like them. I think I should be famous by now. Really. I always thought that by age thirty-four I'd own a home with a yard, not a condo in the city. I still buy all my clothes on sale and I don't like my wardrobe. I say "like" and "awesome" way too much for an adult.

So it's starting to look like we're all in the same boat with this I-should-be-doing-better stuff. Because it's such a universal human issue, maybe we can make a collective pact to stop with the shoulds? Can we all agree to be a little kinder to ourselves? Can we set aside the judgments and be proud of ourselves right this minute, not waiting for when we achieve something we haven't yet achieved?

Here are some ways you can work on dropping the I-should-be-better syndrome and decide you are okay, right now.

1. Understand your own personal flavor of I-should-be-better.

How does this syndrome show up in your life? Are there particular times you are more likely to compare yourself to others? Are there certain skills or habits or traits you are always requiring of yourself? Does it tend to show up primarily in your career, family life, weight issues, or finances? Or is it a theme across the board for you? Is it triggered by particular people (i.e.: that "cool girl" from high school who is now your Facebook friend, or an older sister to whom you were constantly compared)? Understanding how this tendency looks in your life—and being on the lookout for it—is the first step to dropping the habit.

2. Notice. Stop. Breathe.

When you find yourself in the middle of I-should-be-better, stop. Drop what you are doing and take a deep breath. I-should-be-better is cerebral and ego-based. It's your mind spinning stories that aren't real in any factual way. So when you notice those mental stories spinning, stop and consciously shift from being in your mind to being in your body. The fastest and most effective way I know to do that is to breathe deeply and consciously. Notice, stop, and breathe.

3. Remember that you created the rules.

Remind yourself that the standards to which you are holding yourself aren't objective or real. You invented them and you are the only one holding yourself to them. Buying into the standards is simply a habit. With a little intention and awareness, change is not only possible, but very much within your reach.

4. Remind yourself that this is a universal issue.

Just about everyone feels this way at one time or another. It's not only you. We can't all be right–by definition, we can't all be not good enough. If ninety-nine percent of the population should be doing better, isn't it time to change our definition of "good enough?"

5. Are you telling the truth?

How does it feel when you focus on what you should be doing? If what you are telling yourself doesn't feel good, it's probably not the truth. Don't worry—that doesn't make you a liar, it just makes you a perfectly normal human who believes too many painful and unnecessary thoughts. Think about the rules you are setting for yourself: "I should have more money saved" or "I should be further up the corporate ladder." Can you absolutely know for sure that you should? What if you are wrong? What if you are exactly where you should be right now?

6. Look for the lessons.

Look for the lessons in the supposed "mistakes" you've made. Why is it that your kid isn't reading as well as the neighbor kid? Ask this with an open mind, considering all possibilities. Is the neighbor kid extraordinarily gifted? Could your kid simply use a little more practice? This is not an invitation to blame or judge, but an opportunity to look honestly at the situation and your role in it. If there was something you could do differently, what might it be? What can you learn from this nagging sense of I-should-be-better? As long as you are going to insist on being dissatisfied, you might as well learn something from it.

As hard as the I-should-be-better syndrome can be, I actually see it as a sign of deep self-love to believe you deserve good stuff.

Now maybe we can come together in the name of all that self-love and do it without the conditions, without needing to prove our worth through arbitrary accomplishments, and, most importantly, without the shame.

57

Wouldn't THIS by Wild?

What if all humans were equal? Not just created equal…but what if we couldn't help but remain equals our entire lives no matter what happened to us or whatever choices we made?

What if all the evidence we use to separate ourselves from others—all those facts and all that proof that we use to decide that we're better or worse or the same or different—were totally random?

What if our human truths like, "It's better to be this way than that way," were fictional—completely made up and scripted like *Alice in Wonderland* and *Keeping up with the Kardashians?*

What if we were all equally worthy of love? What if rich and poor and fat and thin and happy and depressed and genius and mentally retarded were all okay? Being one instead of the other didn't make you better or worse, it just made you different.

What if those labels were observations rather than judgments—noticing that a person is attractive or schizophrenic or homeless would be just like noticing that you had an apple or a pear or a banana?

Have you ever wondered what things would be like in a world of equality? Have you thought about how we'd treat each other and what we'd chose to do with our lives and how we'd feel when we look in mirror...

Wouldn't that be wild?

58

How to Believe in
Your Positive Qualities

Shadow work is a practice in the self-help world that involves delving into and coming to fully embrace your shadow parts. Your shadow parts are similar to what you might think of as flaws or faults but that's the whole point….they are not flaws. *You are not flawed.* You simply have light and dark, just like everything in the Universe.

Without dark you wouldn't know light and that's not just a cliché. Think about it—if everyone was always good, it would be kind of freaky, wouldn't it? We wouldn't label people or behaviors as "good" or appreciate the positive. Contrast is what makes appreciation of the positive possible.

Anyway, you have shadow parts. And it's okay to get to know them and come to love and accept them as a totally valid part of you.

What we resist persists. So if you try to hide the fact that you are gay, for example, you get caught having sex with men in airport bathrooms. When you try to always appear perfect you become anorexic, and your "imperfections" will be made clear to the world. The shadow will come out and it deserves to; there's nothing wrong with it. So it's always smart to let it out on your own terms.

To me, the most important reason to accept your shadow isn't because it'll come out and screw you if you don't. It's because as long as you are lying to yourself about your shadow, you'll never be able to trust your own judgment.

You'll never be able to truly appreciate your awesomeness because you'll think you can't be trusted. Because you can't accept your shadow, you'll wonder if you can really accept your virtues. I constantly talk to people who are hesitant to accept their awesomeness. We've all been there.

This is why the more you accept your shadow, the easier it is to bask in the light.

59

Compare and Despair

To whom do you compare yourself?

Your neighbor? Your siblings? Who you were ten years ago? The vision of who you thought you would be today that you constructed ten years ago? Who would you be if you were unable to compare yourself with anyone else? This is not a rhetorical question. If you were unable to compare yourself with anyone else, how would your day have been different?

How would your life be different?

Imagine that you wake up tomorrow and think: How strange that Anna compares herself to Rachel. Anna believes that Rachel has it all together and when she compares herself to that image she feels bad about her own life. Anna isn't around when Rachel locks herself in the bathroom and cries or loses her temper with her kids. How strange that Pete feels bad about himself when he looks at Tony. Pete believes he should be more like Tony. He doesn't know the depth of insecurity Tony feels when he compares himself to Dan.

Imagine that you made up a completely arbitrary rule years ago. Maybe it was something like, "I should be funny," or "I should have a full time job," or "I should enjoy spending time with my family." There was no real basis in reality for this rule. You made it up and have probably spent a long time trying to make it feel true.

Then you checked your life against that rule and if there was a mismatch, you decided you weren't good enough.

Imagine that you wake up tomorrow and think that holding yourself to arbitrary rules that you created just doesn't serve you in any positive way.

Maybe you wake up tomorrow believing that to compare yourself to anyone else is completely illogical…you suddenly believe that it isn't a valid comparison so it makes no sense at all to even go there.

Imagine that.

60

You Don't Hate Yourself

I have a client who has uncovered and started to turn around some life-long patterns. She's learned a ton about herself in a month of our working together and has made huge changes in the way she operates in the world. But every time she discovers an unwanted pattern of behavior or way of thinking, she comes back to the same questions: Why am I choosing to suffer? Do I keep doing these things because I want to feel bad?

She's not alone. I frequently hear people attribute their bad habits and painful patterns to:

- Self-sabotage: "I always screw things up."
- Masochism: "I guess I just enjoy suffering on some level."
- Lack of self-love: "The real reason I (procrastinate, drink, keep getting fired, and so on) is because I don't love myself, right?"

I'm not saying that many of us don't self-sabotage to some degree. Our brains don't like drastic change so our subconscious works like a thermostat, trying to keep us at our internal set point. What we call self-sabotage is often just our brain trying to keep homeostasis. But that's not always the case.

It isn't masochism, either.

And I'm definitely not saying we couldn't all benefit from an extra serving of self-love. We surely could.

It's just that it's usually much simpler than all of that. Much of the time if you knew better, you'd do better. Maybe you procrastinate because you are making the task too big, or telling yourself something that scares you into freezing. Maybe you keep getting fired because you are doing something offensive that you are not aware of, or you need more training in your job.

Before we jump into "I-hate-myself-and-suffering-is-familiar-to-me-and-I-don't-deserve-happiness," let's rule out the more practical possibilities first. I don't believe that anyone wants to feel bad. We just don't always know how to feel good. We get stuck in patterns. Our brain gets in its ruts and we don't know that we can get ourselves out by changing our focus or hearing another perspective or calming down enough for your mind to see other options.

So we can all take a deep breath (together now) and stop being so dramatic and taking our stuff so seriously.

Ah, that's better.

You don't hate yourself. You are just stuck in a pattern and you are not sure what to do.

61

Do You Care What
Other People Think of You?

Doing things we don't want to do in order to gain approval from others is an epidemic. Maybe even a pandemic. We aren't dropping dead from it, but we die a little inside each time we make a choice based on what we think will make other people like us.

Why do we care so much? It actually has almost nothing to do with them. It's much more about what we think of ourselves. We let others' opinions determine how we feel about ourselves and operate as if that's the opinion that matters. The self-judgment is what really hurts. We care about what they think because we believe them.

I love this example from Wayne Dyer. I use it all the time: If someone called you a tree, would you care? Would it really bother you if they called you up, screaming, "You are such a Maple, I can't even stand it!" I'm guessing it wouldn't bother you much. You'd know their opinion says something about them, not you. It's in their head, out of their mouth, based on how they view the world. You'd say, "Crazy friend, I'm not a tree!" and go on with your day. You'd shake your head and wonder "What got into him? He's off his rocker."

So why does it bother you so much when they call you a bad singer or a bad employee or a bad friend? Why don't you react the same way as when they call you a tree, knowing their judgment is about them and wondering what they must be going through to think such a thing? Because you know you are not a tree. But when they call you those other things, part of you believes them.

You buy into their story, even if just for a minute. You fear they might be right. That's a big part of why we go out of our way for approval. It doesn't have nearly as much to do with them as it does with us.

This, of course, is good news. Your opinions are something you can work on. Others' opinions? None of your business.

62

Human Mirrors

"Everything that irritates us about another can lead us to an understanding of ourselves."

—Carl Jung

Think about the people who push your buttons and trigger you most: your mom, the nosy neighbor, or that lady in the cubicle next to you who plays Angry Birds all day as if no one is on to her. Think about the feeling you get around these people. Repulsion is common, as is any physical reaction that makes you want to distance yourself from them. Try to pinpoint exactly what bothers you about them.

I have some very bad news for you. That thing that most bothers you about them...it's in you, too. If it weren't, you wouldn't be so emotional about it. For us to recognize traits in others, we have to know those traits. We know them because we have them. On some level, you recognize those traits in yourself and you are fighting like hell to resist them. That's why other people are mirrors for our own stuff.

The cool part is, when you work on those things in yourself you stop seeing them so clearly in others. Let me give you an example.

The wife of a good friend triggers me. When I'm around her I feel like I'd cut off my right arm to make her stop talking and I have a strong urge to take a shower when I get home. Yeah, that's repulsion. It's obvious to me that we're a lot alike. It's not so obvious to other people (I've asked, repeatedly). The traits she openly displays are the ones I also have, but wish I didn't. She makes no excuses for her impatience or for the fact that she's easily bored and jumps from one activity to the next. She's constantly striving for a higher level of success instead of being content in the moment.

I can be like that, too. The difference is, I'm not so okay with those traits all the time. That's not who I want to be.

An interesting thing happened a few months ago. I got really honest with myself about the presence of those traits in me. I admitted that they're there. I sat with them for a while. I embraced them a little more than I had before. I even said, "I love that about me!" when they surfaced over the next few weeks. That was my attempt to make peace with them.

The result: it took a lot of the pressure off. I felt more acceptance and less judgment. I have a sense of where these things come from and I know they're part of me. They aren't good or bad, as much as I was telling myself they were.

The cool part is, the more I allow myself to see these traits in me the less I feel like showering after seeing my friend's wife. When I'm willing to see what she's showing me, I'm not as repulsed by her.

Others people are a mirror, after all. When you are okay with what you see in the mirror, you won't mind sitting in front of one.

63

Give Yourself Some Sound Advice

Do you ever look back at the person you were at some point in the past and think about what you might tell that person now? From who you are today, what would you tell the you of ten years ago?

Ten years ago, I was starting my second year of graduate school. I thought life was something to be taken very seriously. I was an adult and I was on my own in a very real way for the first time. And I was doing serious things that required serious amounts of discipline, responsibility, and focus. Ugh. Just thinking of that time makes my body tense.

I believed without a doubt that the number of academic publications I had to my name would impact the course of my life. I let my PhD advisor's opinion of me matter more than my own opinion of me. I compared myself to my friends who weren't in grad school—they had real jobs and real apartments and real lives, I thought. I worried that I was twenty-three and was only attracted to men who were unavailable or uninterested. That couldn't bode well for my future relationships.

I constructed a lot of rules for myself, thinking that's what it took to succeed. I was doing what I thought would make me happiest but life wasn't nearly as joyful as it could've been. It definitely wasn't lived in the present. As a matter of fact, my life then was kind of lived for today, ten years down the road, and my life today looks nothing like I thought it would. Interesting…

From who I am today, what would I tell that woman of ten years ago? I'd love to have a long talk with her. Here are some of the things I'd say:

- RELAX. You can't do it wrong, really. What you see as failure is not. What you see as success isn't, either.
- Outside of this small little world you are in, no one knows your advisor. Or how many publications he has. And no one will care what he thought of you. Ten years from now, you won't care either.
- Stop preparing and live now. You are already "there."
- Get out of your head. Set aside your beliefs and listen to your body.
- Sit with the discomfort and learn from it. Do what feels good and let your emotions be your guide.
- You rock, by the way. You are doing the best you know how and you are growing so much more than you realize. Life get's good, trust me.

Which made me think…

From ten years into the future, what would I tell the person I am today? I got very quiet and went to that still, inner place that knows. After sitting there for a while, here's what I heard:

- The things you still worry over are all part of the journey. The patterns you keep falling into are simply material to work with—ways that you get to keep growing and help other people along the way. They're a perfect part of the design. Try to be more okay with them.
- Enjoy life. Indulge. Be in the moment. Notice how delicious it is.

- Keep your values front-of-mind. Be with your baby, do even more of what you love. Always let your values guide your actions.
- Enjoy this time of creation. Stop preparing and live now. You are already "there."
- Get out of your head. Set aside your beliefs and listen to your body.
- Sit with the discomfort and learn from it. Do what feels good and let your emotions be your guide.
- You rock, by the way. You are doing the best you know how and you are growing so much more than you realize. Life get's even better, trust me.

What advice would the current you give the former you? What would the future you tell the current you? Are you listening?

64

Fitting In versus Belonging

St. Patrick's Day used to mean drinking all day.

I'm not exaggerating. I'd spend the day with a large group of people—a few real friends and hoards of acquaintances and virtual strangers. We'd start the bar crawl at 7 a.m. on March 17th and end around 2 a.m. on the 18th.

It was fun. At the time, I truly believed partying all day was as good as life could get. I bought into the societal story that as soon as I left college I'd be boxed in, weighed down with responsibility, and forced to resign to what was expected of me. I thought those years in my twenties were the only time I'd really get to be me. After that, I'd have to be one of them.

I had it completely backwards. Just the opposite turned out to be true. These days, St. Patrick's Day is spent dressing up my little girl in shamrocks, drinking a kale and kiwi shake instead of green beer, and spending part of my day in hard core gratitude for the "luck" around me. I'm writing things that reach people, helping brave souls separate fear from facts, and all the while trying to keep my own fictional stories in check.

Boring? Boxed in? Not even close.

I'm not going to lie—there are definitely times when I miss my old life. Sometimes it feels as if it would be easier to numb out than to actually face the lies of "I have to" and "I'm not good enough" that parade through my head daily. When flirting with cute strangers was so much easier than being open and vulnerable in real relationships.

Back then, calling in sick on the 18th meant letting down a corporate boss with whom I felt no real connection…things are very different from now, when a "sick day" means bailing on myself and the unbelievable people I get to serve.

So life might seem harder in some ways now, but it's incredibly natural and much easier in other ways.

I work on staying awake and aware and that's not always easy; but I also get the reward of being me. I'm working on following my own way, not (bar) crawling with a crowd.

Not just feeling like I fit in, but actually belonging in this life I've created.

That's what I call Lucky.

Part V

In Relationship with Others

"Relationships are part of the vast plan for our enlightenment."
—Marianne Williamson

I'm not really sure what the true purpose of relationships is.

I think it has something to do with growing as individuals. Relationships are mirrors that help us see ourselves more clearly. Relationships bring up all our issues and help us to evolve.

And it definitely has a lot to do with love. Relationships give us the opportunity to dive into love and know it from all angles. Feeling it, withholding it, having it and then not having it, and most of all, giving it.

A Course in Miracles says that what hurts us most is not that someone took their love away from us, but that we took our love away from them. Withholding love is the most painful action we can take.

One thing I know about relationships is that most people make them much more difficult and complex than they need to be. We over-think things and we let our fear take over and we become guarded...all of which add layers of complexity that are totally normal and human, but also totally unnecessary.

So here's to peeling back those layers, giving more love than we receive, and making things a whole lot easier on ourselves.

65

The Cast of Characters in Your Life

Every once and a while I talk to someone who asks permission to end a friendship. They say something like, "Is it really okay that I stop calling?", or "I can't just 'break-up' with her...can I?"

Here's my view on relationships:

Life is like a play—there are many scenes and a rotating cast of characters. Some characters are there throughout the entire play. Their roles might change; they might have a leading role in some scenes and a supporting role in others. They might be a background prop in some scenes but they're still there. Others aren't around for long. They might have a starring role in one scene then they exit stage left and don't return.

When you watch a play and notice that a character doesn't come back, there's no judgment. It just is. It's what's in the script and what makes sense in the context of the overall story. New supporting characters come in as the main character (you) evolves. It wouldn't make sense any other way. It wouldn't make sense to have every single character in every single scene simply because they've always been there. They don't need to be there for the mere fact that "We grew up together," or "We've known each other so long."

I understand that in real life there may be emotional attachment when we've known people for a long time. But think about a play. Would it flow as well if every single character stayed around just because they happened to be in the opening scene? Especially if they're not adding to the storyline or supporting the main character anymore?

The characters are not arbitrary. Each one leaves some type of imprint on the main character (you). Characters are never written in without a purpose. The purpose might be to teach the main character something important, highlight her personality in some way, serve as contrast, or their role might be as life-long friend or soul mate.

There may be a person who was once your number one BFF until things change. That's a massively important character whose impact does not fade when the character exits the stage. The imprint has been made on the main character (you) and that imprint lasts throughout the entire play.

Every character has a purpose. This is often especially true of the ones that aren't around for long. Writing them into scene after scene even when the storyline has changed just doesn't make sense. It's okay to let some characters exit your life.

66

The Relationship Manual

It's amazing how furious we can get about how others treat us.

A friend was complaining that her boyfriend wasn't thoughtful enough to have her favorite wine on hand for their anniversary dinner. She never mentioned wanting it. It's a red and they were having seafood. But in her mind, it was a total no-brainer. He's obviously not a thoughtful guy.

A client believed her friends "should have known" she'd need to spend the entire girls-night-out venting about her boss. I asked if she forgot to give them The Manual. When she got defensive and demanded to know what The Manual is, I explained: It sounds like you expect people to know what you want and how you want to be treated. There must be some kind of instruction manual you've written and shared with them. Maybe they just haven't read it yet.

I learned about The Manual from one of my mentors, life coach Brooke Castillo. It's brilliant, and so right on. How often do we expect others to read our minds, anticipate our needs, think the way we think, and act the way we would act?

Constantly.

We expect others to take care of us but we're not taking care of ourselves at all. We put it all on them, as if our happiness is their job.

I once had a person write into my relationship advice column wanting to know what she should do about the guy she'd been dating. She said he didn't want to pick her up for their dates. On their first three dates, they met each other out. She drove on their fourth date—she offered to drive, and he accepted. He came to her house for dinner on their fifth date. So, in five dates he hadn't picked her up and driven her anywhere.

Her conclusion? He was obviously extremely rude and not a gentleman at all. On top of that, he wasn't putting any effort into the dates or into impressing her, which clearly meant that he wasn't interested in her, anyway.

Clearly.

She didn't write to me seeking clarification or for an outside perspective on his behavior, but to ask how she should dump him. Should she dump him outright or should she confront him on all of these terrible things he did first, and then dump him?

I suggested that maybe he liked her so much that he was embarrassed he didn't have a nicer car. Or maybe he wanted to be so respectful that he thought meeting on neutral ground for their first few dates was the proper thing to do. Or maybe he didn't want to drive for any number of reasons but he was still a wonderful person who she might go on to have a loving, long-term relationship with if she could move past her own rigid judgments. None of these options had ever occurred to her. She was absolutely positive that her read of this guy was spot on. Apparently, he never read her manual either.

Please don't assume people know what you want if you haven't explicitly told them. And even when you have explicitly told them, try not to assume they heard you the way you meant to be heard.

Communicate if you have doubts. Clarify, ask for what you want, and elaborate on what you want. Needing to ask for what you want doesn't mean that the other person isn't a match because they "should have known." They shouldn't have known, ever.

Cut them some slack and don't expect them to read your mind. Or your manual.

67

Dealing with People the Enlightened Way: Agenda-Free

Let's say, for example, you've started dabbling in Enlightenment. You've embraced your power and dropped the victim stuff. You realize you are responsible for your own happiness and while others make your life better, you don't need them to have a better life.

A common issue often comes up at this point. How do you handle it when someone does something that really bothers you? You are more Enlightened than you used to be but you are still human. Things are going to bother you.

Sometimes you can simply walk away. That's a pretty Enlightened response, when you can do it. Turn the other cheek. But that doesn't always work. Sometimes if you bite your tongue you feel inauthentic. It feels like being a kid again or being told your opinions don't matter.

So if you decide that the best course of action is to say something, keep this in mind to help you do it in an Enlightened way: Have no agenda.

You are speaking your mind for the sake of being honest and authentic. There is no other agenda. You are not trying to change them. You are not trying to influence them. You are saying how you feel in the most kind and loving and non-threatening way possible.

Then, you step back and totally let them have their reaction. How they react, what they think, and what they do as a result...none of your business. No agenda. Their opinions are just as valid as yours, so there's nothing to change about them, anyway.

No agenda because you are too Enlightened to waste your energy arguing with reality. You got to express your reality; let them keep theirs.

68

The Quest to Figure Them Out

We all try to interpret the words and actions of other people. We do it partly because we're curious, armchair psychologists. It's interesting to ponder others' inner workings

"Why would she do that?"—said by everyone on earth, at some point.

"What did he mean by that thing he said?"—said by anyone with a pulse and heartbeat.

But this quest for answers is not always innocent curiosity. It's not always agenda-free. In fact, it's usually very agenda-laden. It's usually our way of trying to control things. If we can figure them out, we can change them. If we can get in their head, we have a better chance of getting what we want.

Except that never works. Never.

Notice how much time you spend wondering why someone did or said what they did or said. How much time you spend in their business, playing detective, making assumptions, and formulating theories?

Then notice how it feels when you try to figure them out. Does it feel good? Seriously, is it fun and interesting in the armchair psychologist way? Or is it frustrating and confusing, like struggling with an impossible puzzle?

You would think it would feel good to know what they're thinking and that's what drives you to try to figure it out. But does the process of analyzing them actually feel good? If you are like most of us, it doesn't feel good. And if that's the case, might I suggest letting that go?

Let them be them and if you must worry about something worry about your own motivations. Rather than devoting your energy to solving the unsolvable or changing the unchangeable, marvel in reality and operate from there.

Accept what they did or said at face value, and then move on. Channel your energy toward something you might benefit in understanding. Something you can perhaps change.

Something like You.

69

A Cure for Envy

I'm experimenting with a new theory about a way to transform envy. Because feeling envy isn't fun and I know there has to be a more Enlightened way.

How do you react when your envy is triggered? Here's how I react:

I'm a little jealous of this awesome woman I know. I feel it when she updates her Facebook status with the things she's doing that I want to be doing. I immediately compare my plans to hers. That's mistake number one.

Then, I start looking for her flaws in a desperate attempt to feel better. What's so special about her? But that doesn't work because judging other people never feels good, even when you come out on top. Because I'm feeling bad from judging her, it's easy to fall into judging myself. What's so wrong with me? Don't I deserve what she has? Maybe if I had worked a little harder, been a little nicer, was smarter or prettier…

It's a vicious game of ego ping-pong. I'm better. No, she's better. No, I'm better.

Comparison. Self-judgment. Other-judgment. Life isn't fair. None of this is cool, so what to do instead?

Flip It

As a general rule, the fastest and most extreme way to change how you feel is to flip it on its head. When you flip judging them and questioning their entitlement on its head, what do you get?

Celebrate them. Believe that they deserve all the blessings that come their way. I know it's not natural. It's going to take some effort and it'll probably feel fake at first. But if you stick with it, it could really transform things.

I first tried flipping it when I couldn't get pregnant. At that time, I worked in downtown Chicago on the same block as the busiest labor and delivery hospital in the city. Every day at lunch I'd walk past five or twenty or fifty or so pregnant women going in for appointments or waddling in to have their babies. I'd see their friends and family walking excitedly down the street with "It's a Boy!" balloons bobbing above their heads.

For a while, I let those sightings trigger thoughts of what I didn't have. I allowed those women to set a whole It's-not-fair-why-her-and-not-me tirade into motion. Then I came across a trick for getting what you want, based on the principle of appreciating what you want wherever you see it, even if it's not in your own life. It's based on the basic truth that we all have every human potential and possibility within us. If it's possible for one person to think or feel or experience something, it's possible for you, too.

So I decided to start celebrating the pregnant women. I figured that if everything that's in them is also in me (a baby, somewhere)—and if you get more of what you appreciate—it just might be a really smart thing to try. Besides, I was desperate for a way to go out for coffee without becoming jealous and pissed at the universe.

I'd look at the pregnant women and think "You go, girl!" "Good for you!" "Congratulations!" I started smiling at them. I even asked one very large woman when she was due. That may not sound like a big deal to you but it was huge for me.

It didn't feel natural at first and it certainly wasn't my default response. So I stayed as conscious and aware as possible so that I was poised to choose my thoughts instead of revert to the default.

When the automatic, default envy crept up, I just flipped it around and celebrated them as soon as I could muster it. It's never too late to change course. After a while, it became easier. I treated pregnancy like a secret society that I was about to join. I started getting excited to see a pregnant lady because I could give her the big smile and secret nod that said, "Good for you! I'm on my way there, too."

My optimism about my own situation improved. Most of all, I simply felt nicer. Not so much like a victim, less like things were unfair, and more like I could do what I wanted with this obstacle. That was my early experience with this envy transformation tool. I think it's time to dust it off and start using it again.

While my Facebook friend is speaking at a TED conference or biking through wine country and I'm facing a night of dirty diapers and laundry, I'm going to try my best to genuinely celebrate her. I tell myself: This is where I am right now and that's where she is right now. Things are always changing. And seriously, good for her for having such an awesome life. It has nothing to do with me.

If anything, the fact that she can do it proves that I can, too. The more I celebrate her, the more room I allow for what she has to show up in my life. Jealousy is resistance and resistance doesn't attract, it repels. Ultimately, the happier I am for her, the happier I can be for me. So I'm experimenting with that. Doesn't it seem as if the people who celebrate others usually end up doing pretty well themselves?

I think it just might work.

70

When Your Parent Can't
Give You the Love You Deserve

I knew I'd write about this someday, but it wasn't supposed to be now. Then a friend confided in me that she was scared to death that her mother—who doesn't show her much love or approval—was right about her. And someone else turned to me when her relationship with her parents unraveled because they couldn't accept some of her lifestyle choices.

I have a rule that if the Universe brings something to my attention more than once, I listen. So here we are. This issue takes many forms. Sometimes your parent can't show unconditional love because of their own mental, emotional or substance abuse issues. Sometimes they seemingly could love and accept you if they wanted to, but they can't find the courage to forgive, or tell the truth, or do the hard work it sometimes takes to make a relationship work.

Maybe your parent is technically still in your life but not in your life in any meaningful way. You just don't seem to relate to each other or connect the way you'd like. Or maybe they've died. Or maybe they've stopped speaking to you altogether. They might even ignore your calls and choose to have no relationship at all. I'm in the latter camp.

It sucks when your parent disapproves, regardless of the circumstances. It does not matter how old you are or how many of your own children you've raised.

It does not matter how mentally suspect said parent is. It doesn't even matter that you coach people through relationship issues, or that those people often claim that you've helped them repair their relationships. Sometimes you still can't repair your own.

As I know from having dealt with this for some time now—and as you know if you've been dealing with it, too—there are many aspects of this difficult situation that take their turn in the spotlight.

Here are some common issues of this situation that really suck:

1. The Part about Believing Them.

We're biologically wired to look to our parents for information about who we are. That natural tendency to base our identity on what our parents think never completely goes away. As adults, we realize our parents' judgment isn't foolproof. Their perception is colored by their own painful history or poor choices. But innocent little kids don't know this. Mommy and Daddy have to be trustworthy and all-knowing; if they're not, our safety and survival are in danger. By the time we're old enough to see the truth, we already have years of experience believing them. The mental rut is worn; the habit well-cemented. So even if you've created a fabulous life for yourself and you are proud of who you are; even if you've learned to love yourself and truly believe in your own worth as much as is humanly possible…when mom or dad disapproves, you are going to question yourself for at least a second, maybe longer—usually longer. You are going to temporarily set aside everything you know and love about yourself and automatically believe your parent. You'll wonder, "Are they right about me?" no matter how absurd their opinion may be.

But then, if you are blessed with the gift of awareness (or if you work hard to foster it), you can refocus and listen to your own judgment. You can remember, "Oh yeah, mom and dad don't know me the way I know me. They have their own stuff going on and that's what makes them see things the way they do. I don't need them for my survival or my identity anymore." So, a big part of what hurts when a parent disapproves of you is that you question yourself, always, for a while. But don't worry—the length of the "while" gets shorter and shorter with time and practice.

2. The Part About It Being Unfair.

At some point, you realize your parents have issues of their own that drive them to be the way they are. Then, if you are anything like me, you get pissed as well as sad and disappointed. You feel robbed of the kind of parent you deserve, and it's not fair. It hurts to see our parents' humanity. Life was so much easier when we were kids and we could inherently trust them. We had someone to look up to—mom and dad were our heroes. They were the best.

We feel the loss as an adult. It's not fair that other adults can turn to their parents for advice throughout their lives and that they always have a solid, reliable place to turn to for protection and support. Parents are supposed to love and accept their children no matter what, to be their biggest cheerleaders, always be proud, brag to their friends, and want to see their children have a better life than they had. Except sometimes they don't. And that hurts. If you are in this situation, feel each and every emotion as it comes up. They're all okay. They are totally human, totally acceptable. They will fade, and they fade faster when you allow yourself to feel what you feel. You don't need more judgment in your life so don't judge yourself for how you feel. Drop the judgment and accept where you are.

3. The Part About Being Afraid You Are Like Them.

Personality equals genes plus environment, right? You have their genes and they've been your environment since day one. Rest assured, you won't wake up one day and find that you suddenly and magically are your mom. You may wake up one day and start using her phrases, or you might look in the mirror one day to see her gray hair or crow's-feet. But you won't suddenly wake up with her insecurities, her cynicism, or her negative outlook on life. It doesn't work that way.

In fact, with a little conscious focus on your part, you can achieve just the opposite.

When we experience anything we don't want, that experience sets into motion a desire for what we do want. Crap encourages clarity.

Your relationship with your parent will undoubtedly shape you; but you get to determine how it shapes you.

Compassion

I'm sorry my dad had bad stuff show up in his life. I'm sorry that he hasn't found a way to have easy, happy relationships. He simply doesn't know how, and that's no different from how I don't know how to speak Mandarin. Sometimes I think he could have figured it out if he really wanted to. If he were stronger or more courageous or more motivated, maybe he could have gotten some help and worked on his stuff and things would be different.

When I think that I get angry and it's really difficult to muster compassion through anger. The point is, there are times when compassion isn't possible and that's totally okay.

But when you can muster it, compassion is the antidote. Like forgiveness, you offer compassion because it makes you feel good. It has little to do with them. It's not like they even know what you are doing anyway. They're somewhere else, in the middle of their own stuff. You offer compassion in your mind, generate it in your body, and wish it onto them. And it heals you.

As a parent myself, there's one thing I know for sure: No one would choose to have a horrible relationship with their children if they saw a reasonable way out. I also know this for sure: it has to feel like pure hell to withhold your love from your children and grandchildren. I can definitely have compassion for anyone in that situation.

Thanks

I also thank my dad, and that heals me. I'm grateful to him for trying when he did because I know that couldn't have been easy on him. I'm grateful to him for being there when he was, because it wasn't always this way. And I'm grateful for this relationship, exactly as it is.

This painful situation has made me a better wife, mother, daughter, sister, and friend. The deep disappointment I feel is what fuels my passion for the radically different kind of relationship I'm building with my own child.

And that's a really, really good thing.

My gratitude doesn't mean I wouldn't change it all in a second if I could. But it does make it easier to feel compassion and unconditional love for my dad, and for this rotten situation.

71

Are You Keeping Score?

If you are playing to win in your relationship, you've already lost.

When you are keeping score or playing to win you are like a prosecuting attorney, constantly putting your partner on trial and building your case against them.

To build your case, you have to be chronically tuned into to what's wrong instead of what's right. You are always looking for things they did to you. Although you are the prosecutor, you are defensive as hell.

When you are looking for what's wrong, you are going to find it. That's how the mind works—it concocts stories and spins facts so that what you see conveniently matches what you are looking for.

The Score-Keepers

Score-keepers aren't selfish, unkind, or egotistical. They're usually just afraid. They're afraid of the vulnerability that comes hand-in-hand with close relationships, and rightfully so. They're always on the lookout for where they might have been wronged; always on the defense. They desperately want to trust and appreciate their partner, but they find it much more difficult than the average person. They're skeptical because they're afraid of being hurt.

Score-keepers are not bad people; they're just operating from full-on self-protection mode which is why they devote so much energy to indicting the people they love.

Score-keepers often rely on their partner or their relationship to make them feel good. When that relationship is the primary source of their sense of love and belonging, they have a lot to lose. So score-keepers police their partners as a way of trying to ensure their own happiness.

Except that the vigilance doesn't work.

If you are a score-keeper and you are not sure how else to be, let's look at the alternative. Non-score-keepers assume the best about others. They are trusting and not skeptical. They don't go looking for problems and because they're not looking, they very rarely find them.

They don't feel driven to stay vigilant to the offenses against them because they have a deeper sense of self-worth that's not tied to their partner. Perhaps they were never told, "You can't trust anyone but yourself," so they don't subscribe to that particular lie.

They can let go and trust that things will be fine because they actually believe that they will be. Sure, they have fears and insecurities like all humans, but deep down they know they'll be fine no matter what happens. There is no reason to keep score because there is nothing they need protection from.

If You are a Score-Keeper

Don't worry if the description of a score-keeper describes you. You can change your ways and dramatically improve your relationship by simply being aware when you find yourself building your case against your partner. Recognize when you feel yourself shift into prosecutor mode and simply ease up a little. Whatever it is that has offended you, you can practice letting it go.

Remember that noticing and punishing these wrongdoings is just a habit you've come to adopt out of fear, but that it really doesn't protect you at all. It achieves just the opposite, actually. This behavior is not who you are; it's simply what you do. There's a huge difference.

Remind yourself that all is well. If you don't believe it at first, practice saying it anyway. All is well. There is nothing you have to do in order to stay safe. You are already safe—the fear you feel is natural and we all feel it at times, but it's not real. Keep in mind that although keeping score feels like it's keeping you safe, it's actually hurting you. It's much safer to let go and trust. Acknowledging your fear and trusting anyway is what gives your relationship its best chance at survival.

72

The Real "Rules" for a
Good Relationship

How many relationship rules have you heard in your life? Too many to count, I'd bet.

- Wait three days before calling.
- Laugh at his jokes and act very interested.
- Tell him you have plans (even when you don't) and act disinterested.
- Don't drink too much, talk about your ex, or have sex on the first date.

The underlying message in all of these rules is, "ignore what you want and who you really are and play a role in the hope that that's what he wants to see."

Really? As if that's going to help you find true love?

How could anyone ever find "true" love when they're not telling the truth? The Rules—whether they're the ones made famous by that book in the 90s or the random adages you heard from Aunt Betty—are not helpful if they're not consistent with your own internal compass.

If you are doing anything only because you think you should or because someone told you to, you are not going to end up with the kind of relationship you are looking for. Lying means your relationship is built on lies. It can't be any other way.

Sure, playing hard to get might seem exciting to some guys and they might ask you out once or twice. But as soon as you get tired of playing and pretending, your true self will come through and the jig will be up.

This all seems painfully clear and obvious to me now. But I remember a time when I was younger and single and just a little insecure and utterly baffled by men and relationships. I was desperate for any information that would help me crack the relationship code. Although masking my true self and ignoring my desires felt wrong, I was willing to try it. I mean, the book was a bestseller for crying out loud. There had to be something more I could learn.

I was willing to give misrepresenting-myself-to-fit-someone-else's-needs a shot. If you are in that place now, it's okay to go along with that particular dating game. It might even be a rite of passage. I can tell you how it will end but you probably don't want to hear it.

We all feel vulnerable in relationships. We're all afraid to reveal ourselves to another person and be honest and open and put ourselves out there for potential rejection. That's why it's so easy to buy into artificial rules that allow you to hide.

But those kinds of rules don't work. The only way you are going to end up in an honest, sustainable relationship is to be You from the beginning. If I were starting all over, I'd make that my only rule.

When you think about it, it really doesn't get much easier than that.

73

Is There Something Wrong with Your Relationship? Or is it You?

Relationships are kind of like therapy—they bring all your dirt to the surface so you can work through it and move beyond it. This makes perfect sense because relationships and therapy have the same purpose: growth.

Therapy is especially hard in the beginning because you are becoming aware of all the dirt you've been hiding under the surface for so long. Therapy doesn't create the dirt; it just exposes it to the light.

It's the same with relationships, except the timing is a little different. Relationships are usually great in the beginning while you are still seeing your new love in their best possible light. You are seeing them as the greatest, most perfect version of themselves. And they see you that way, too.

Eventually something happens and the two of you no longer see each other as that greatest version of yourselves—at least not consistently. They start noticing and then focusing on your flaws. You start focusing on your flaws, too. When you are down about your own flaws, your ego tries to make you feel better by pointing out all your partner's flaws. It's a big, nasty cycle. Suddenly you are tuned in to what's wrong instead of what's right. Your insecurities light up like neon signs. Fear seeps through the cracks because you think you "have" something you could possibly lose. You start all kinds of self-protective behaviors that feel totally necessary (but are always counter-productive) like keeping score, guarding your emotions, and holding back.

I don't have to tell you that none of this feels good. It feels pretty miserable, actually.

Because engaging in these behaviors feels so awful, you say (and begin to believe) the relationship feels awful. This is where I want to save you from throwing away a perfectly good relationship, so listen up: It's not the relationship that feels awful; that's just the pain of personal growth.

Growth almost always hurts in the beginning. Facing dirt is hard and that's what this relationship is doing for you—highlighting your dirt and helping you grow. But it's not only *this* relationship. Any relationship will do that to you. Or, better said, *any relationship will do that for you.*

It's not your partner's fault. It's not that you are not a good match. It's not that this isn't "meant to be." It's that you are faced with the same opportunity for growth you would be facing in any good relationship and that's scary. It's hard. It's easier to walk away.

It's always easier to walk away than it is to grow. Always has been, always will be. So please don't blame the relationship. And for heaven's sake, don't blame yourself or your partner. Just know that this is what growth feels like. Work through the insecurities that come up. Ask yourself the hard questions, like why you are feeling jealous or scared or vulnerable and if you really have to act on those emotions. Realize you can experience all of that dirt and still stick around.

When you work through the dirt and then take the opportunity to clean it up, you are growing.

Part VI

Tapping into Something Bigger

"We don't attract what we want, we attract what we are."
—Wayne Dyer

You know we're all connected, right? Everything in the universe, that is. We are bound together by invisible forces, energy, vibes, what have you...

I bet you've seen that when you ask for things, you often receive them. You might always receive them, it's just that recognizing when you do can be tricky.

And when you are a match for what you want, you get more of it. You end up with things and experiences that line up with your energy.

There's a lot of magic happening every day in the world. Actually, it's not really magic—I believe there's a scientific explanation for everything—we just don't have that explanation yet so it feels like magic.

As cool as science, discovery, and understanding are, it is fun to play with magic, too.

This section is about those things that feel like magic—practical, reliable, and predictable magic.

74

Signs from the Universe

If you've ever had coaching from me, you have probably heard me talk about sticks and birds.

In the practice of setting intentions and creating outcomes in your life, it's common to go through a period where you have a lot of near misses. You put out the intention for more money and find out you are getting an unexpected check for $1,000.00, only to have your car break down and require a $1,001.00 repair. Or you set an intention for having more clients and three new ones call to sign up, only to cancel or change their minds before the first session.

Near misses are really frustrating.

Like many people, I used to prefer nothing to a near miss. Why get my hopes up for something that ultimately doesn't pan out? The fall from that excited place is much harder than the fall from a place of already being disappointed. I used to take near misses as a sign that I was way off track. "Silly girl," the Universe was laughing behind my back, "who are you to get what you want?"

Until I heard about sticks and birds, and then I realized that I had it all backwards. Near misses are signs from the Universe that you are on the right track, not the wrong one. Ms. U is not laughing at you at all; she's showing you that maybe your intention was a little off, or maybe you are not quite ready for what you think you want, but you are close. You are on your way. Just because you can't see it yet doesn't mean it's not right there. And just because it doesn't show up in the exact way you requested doesn't mean you are not still getting what you want.

The sticks and birds story comes from back in the day before GPS technology, when explorers were out at sea for long periods of time not knowing when they might find land. Sticks and birds were visible signs that land was near—they would see sticks floating in the water and birds flying around a few days before they could see the actual land. Although what they wanted hadn't shown up in physical reality yet, it was close. The sticks and birds assured them it was right around the corner.

A few years ago I was going through a medicated fertility cycle and needed to give myself shots at home every night and then go to the doctor daily to have an ultrasound and blood draw. It was loads of fun, let me tell you. But, things were looking great this time around. The follicles were there. My hormone levels looked good. This was not my first time through fertility treatment, but it would be my last for a while if it didn't result in pregnancy—the doctors said my body needed a break from the drugs and stress, and if this particular treatment wasn't successful after a few trials it probably wouldn't be. The next step was much more invasive than nightly shots and daily blood draws.

I was doing my work. I was spending a lot of time each day in meditation and visualizing the medication doing what we wanted it to do. I had incredibly low levels of stress. All the signs were good.

And then, as we were pulling out of the driveway on the night before Thanksgiving on our way to see my in-laws and the eleven kids in their very fertile family, the doctor called and said something was wrong. It wasn't working after all. I'd like to say I reminded myself of sticks and birds and had a wonderful weekend, but that's not at all how it happened. I hated the Universe that night. But I woke up the next day and eventually chose to see it the sticks and birds way. Because what choice did I have, really? That way felt better and I convinced myself that I still deserved to feel good, wonky ovaries and all.

I have a client who has hated his job for a year. He hired me to help him find a new direction. We've worked together to uncover what his real passions are, what he really wants to do instead of what's practical or safe. He's sent out many resumes, networked like crazy, and had about a dozen interviews in our time together. Then he found The One: The Dream Job.

It was going great. He was still interviewing, but they were courting him. We both would have bet large sums of money that he had it nailed. We celebrated together, just waiting for the official offer. Then they changed their mind about the position. Near misses suck. But instead of judging himself for being in pain he met himself where he was. He set aside six hours to feel sorry for himself. I asked him to contain his self-pity and fully feel it during that time and he did it like a champ. I thought he might take a few days but he wanted to do it in six hours.

Then he took a sick day from his dreaded job and did things that he truly loves but never allows himself. They were little things, like walking around the gourmet grocery story in the middle of the day and rollerblading along the lake. He woke up the next day and chose to see his situation the sticks and birds way. He felt better and although he hates his job, he knows he still deserves to feel good. I was a very proud coach.

As for my own sticks and birds story...I eventually followed my doctor's orders and gave my body a much-needed break. After a couple months of detox and focusing on the other parts of my life, I was somehow able to release the desire to control it all. More than I previously had, anyway. I embraced the sticks and birds idea and got myself to a place of faith, where I absolutely knew I'd have what I wanted when and how the Universe wanted to deliver it. It might not look the way I wanted it to and it wasn't happening in my timeframe, but I knew it would happen, one way or another.

I got pregnant the next month with no drugs, no interventions, and no trying to control it. I guess my near miss really was a sign that I was on the right track all along.

75

Ask and You Shall Receive

I wasn't feeling great the other day, and went for a walk. I was filled with worry and self-judgment. I had done some self-coaching that morning but it wasn't giving me the relief I was looking for.

The worry was about having a hard time getting pregnant a second time. I was working with a new fertility client who was struggling in much the same way I once had, and that was triggering a lot my own fears. The self-judgment came from falling into an old pattern I thought I had overcome. I relapsed–it happens. Although I wouldn't judge others for it, I was judging the hell out of myself.

I asked the small, still voice what I might do to feel better. "Wordless" popped into my mind. I was too verbal, too in my head, and could benefit from some silence. So I took my baby for a long walk. As we started out, I set an intention for the walk: "I intend to receive a sign that helps me get out of this funk today." I end all of my intentions with: "This or something better for the greatest good of all involved." Saying this acknowledges that my intentions are set from my limited perspective and what I *really* want may not be what I *think* I want. Ultimately, what I always want is the greatest good for all involved.

Following my intention I say, "Thanks, I quit." I got this part from Martha Beck's *Steering by Starlight*. It's a reminder that we don't need to beg or ask repeatedly for what we want. It's enough to ask once, trust that it's taken care of, and then drop it.

I walked wordlessly for a long time, mostly looking up at the trees and the sky. When I finally peeked down in the stroller, I noticed the baby had dropped her toy. It was her favorite one, or else I probably would have kept going. So we turned around and backtracked, this time scanning the sidewalk for Willow's fuzzy giraffe.

And then I stepped on it. Not the giraffe, but a manhole cover that had the words "FORGIVE YOURSELF" spray-painted across it in huge white letters. Seriously. I had stepped right over it five minutes earlier, but Willow just happened to drop her giraffe and I had to go back. (We eventually found the giraffe, by the way).

We walked for another hour or so before packing up the stroller to drive home. On the way home, I stopped at a red light, and a new billboard caught my eye. I think it was an advertisement for a non-profit that helps with adoption, but I can't be sure. Over a picture of a couple holding a new baby it said, "You will have a baby sooner than you think."

Maybe you'd like to try asking for a sign next time you want a little guidance?

76

A Love Story about Signs

Here's one more story of what happened when I asked for a sign to help me make a decision. This story takes place in 1998. It's a love story.

I was in my last year of undergrad work at Michigan State, and in the process of applying to graduate schools. Because of the specific topics I wanted to study, there were only a handful of appropriate programs to consider. Each of them admitted maybe two or three students each year. I didn't have a ton of options. I applied to eight programs and was accepted into two. Miracle of all miracles, the two that accepted me were my top two choices: Indiana University and University of Virginia.

I visited IU first and loved it. Then I went to UVA and loved that, too. I drove home from Virginia, completely torn. I spent nine hours of driving alone from Virginia to Michigan, thinking, "How am I going to make this decision?"

At that point in my life, the way I made decisions was to make long pro and con lists, or to ask someone smarter for advice, or to look outside of myself and hope that Universe or God or Krishna or someone would drop an answer in my path if they deemed me worthy. I decided on that long drive that I would go home and let myself rest for a day. Then, the following day, I would get a sign that would give me my answer.

I went home and slept. When I woke up and turned on the TV there was my sign. Bobby Knight, wearing a big ol' red and white Indiana sweatshirt, was in a commercial. The commercial was beginning just as I turned the TV on, early in the morning on the day I was expecting it.

So I went to Indiana.

(Truth be told, that's where I really wanted to go and I knew it all along. If I had known enough to listen to my gut, I would have made that choice immediately and saved myself a lot of debate. But I didn't think I could actually trust my gut. My mind wanted me to do due diligence and reason it out rather than feel it out. My mind wanted absolute certainty and I believed that must come from something out there rather than from me simply deciding I was certain.)

Anyway, I went to Indiana. But that's only half of the story. This is where it gets all sappy and romantic.

A couple years later and halfway across the Midwest, my future hubby was considering a move to Indiana for work. He, too, was looking for a sign that it was the right choice for him. He, too, turned on the TV. He watched the show *Home Improvement* —the one with Tim Allen. The storyline of that episode was that the family was moving because Tim's wife, Jill, was going to graduate school. For psychology. At Indiana University.

They packed up and moved from Detroit to Bloomington so that Jill could study psychology. Just like I did.

And future hubby packed up and moved there, too. The rest is history, all because we followed our signs.

77

Something Freaky is Going On

I heart loving-kindness. If you try it, I bet you will too.

When I first started practicing the lovey-dovey ritual, stuff started happening that really freaked me out—in a good way. That's what I want to tell you about. People began looking at me differently, being much friendlier, and calling or emailing out of nowhere after I had sent some love their way.

Those are just some of my experiences—research on practicing compassion tells an even better story. The overwhelming feeling of oneness that you know well if you are a loving-kindness junkie is explained because compassion triggers increased activity in the areas of the brain that produce wellbeing and happiness and decreased activity in the areas that perceive boundaries between oneself and the rest of the world.

So before I dive into some of the crazy stuff that resulted from my sending love to unsuspecting friends and strangers, let me share the basics of my practice so you can start your own.

The Practice

Like many things, there's no clear "right" or "wrong" when it comes to practicing loving-kindness. There are various methods but none of them have to be followed to the letter. If it feels good, you are doing it right. The idea is to generate feelings of love and compassion, feel them yourself, and then project them toward others. I begin by seeing myself surrounded by a bright light. I try to create the feeling of being consumed—enveloped almost—by the light. Then I offer myself compassion.

The wording I originally learned was: "May I be well; May I be happy; May I be free from suffering." Remember, *the exact language you use does not matter*. For awhile I said: "May I be well; May I be happy; May I have everything my heart desires," because I didn't like the word 'suffering' hanging out in the middle of my meditation. Now, 'suffering' doesn't bother me so much so I've gone back to the original form. Again, the exact wording doesn't matter. All that matters is that you say something that feels good to you.

After offering this loving-kindness to myself…and I should say, not just offering it but receiving it and really allowing myself to feel it, I send it to others. I recommend starting with people you already love. It's usually easy to offer loving-kindness to babies and pets; it gets a little messier with complex, speaking adults. So start small and make it easy on yourself.

Think of your cat or your newborn nephew or your closest friend that you are not mad at and picture them hugged by the light. Generate as strong a feeling of love and compassion as you can and let yourself really feel it for a minute (this is where the benefit to you comes in). Then give it away. Transfer all that love you feel onto them and wish them well. "May you be well; May you be happy; May you be free from suffering."

Once you've hit your A-list, start searching for people you know less intimately. You could visually go down the hallway at work focusing on the person in each cubicle, or mentally scroll through your list of Facebook friends. Pick a handful of people and offer them compassion. "May you be well; May you be happy; May you be free from suffering."

Eventually—and this is where it becomes difficult, but most powerful—move on to people you don't love so much. Picture that person who annoys you, or the family member who endlessly judges you, or the person from your past you've never managed to forgive. Try it with someone you feel jealousy toward or someone who has purposely hurt you.

See them clearly in your mind…this alone can be painful. Now, feel all that love and compassion you just offered your adorable new kitten and give it to your enemy, too. See that person as clearly as you can; see them basking in the love you are sending. Wish them well and sincerely hope they are free of suffering.

It's hard at first, but it gets easier—and easier, and easier, until you can actually picture this person in your meditation and effortlessly offer them compassion. Before you know it, you'll be able to think of them in your everyday life without that awful feeling in the pit of your stomach. You ruminate less and accept them more. The resentment begins to fade. The best part is that this has nothing to do with them. They have no idea that you are falling in love with them each night. You get all the benefits.

But loving-kindness is not just for the privacy of your own home. Far from it. My favorite way to practice compassion is to take it to the streets. I offer loving-kindness to people on the train, at Target, and especially in big crowds. You can send the love out into the masses, but I like to focus on just one person at a time and pick a lucky victim out of a crowd. I'll focus on the chosen one, feel the compassion and what it's like to be hugged by the light, and then throw all that mushy love and compassion their way. I'll wish them well, tell them they look nice, that I like their hair, that they deserve everything their heart desires, and that I love them. I do this silently, of course.

The Freaky Stuff

Sometimes when I'm at Target or on the train and I'm sending some stranger love vibes, nothing noticeable happens. I feel it (and it's awesome) and I'm probably smiling to myself like a crazy lady, but sometimes nothing noticeable is going on. And that's fine. It's not disappointing because I'm not doing it for a reaction; I'm doing it because it feels so damn good to me. Once you get over the initial weird factor and you are really starting to generate compassion, you melt into the feeling. You are high on love. Although the practice is focused toward others, it's purely selfish.

What often happens is that the person feels it. They look my way. They smile. On occasion they say hello and once a complete stranger started a conversation. It's not as simple as the fact that they can feel me staring at them the way we all can. That may be part of it, but that's not the whole story because when you stare at someone on the train in Chicago, you don't usually get smiles in return. And you certainly don't get a nod or a hello.

So although I've never asked any of my targets what made them want to connect with me, I'm fairly certain that on some level they felt the love.

When I first started a loving-kindness practice I found that people began to engage with me more during the day. One of the most notable examples was the guy who works at the dry cleaner at the end of my block. Most days when I walk by with my dogs, we wave or smile at each other and maybe exchange an occasional, "Good morning," if he happens to be sitting outside.

One night I decided to focus on him in my meditation. I sent him loving-kindness for a good ten minutes. The next day, as I approached the dry cleaner window on my dog walk, I could see him spot me coming, jump up, and go to the door. Waiting in the doorway, he struck up what turned into about a ten minute conversation. He was suddenly interested in my dogs' names, how long we've been in the neighborhood, where we came from, and so on. It felt both totally out of the ordinary and also very natural and almost expected.

Another string of freaky events took place at the airport. My black-berry died in the cab on the way to the airport and my books were in the trunk, leaving me nothing to do on the drive but meditate. I offered compassion to the cab driver and to people in surrounding cars for most of the thirty minute trip. Once I got into the airport, I noticed that people were staring at me; I even ducked into the restroom to make sure my shirt wasn't see-through.

In the long security line, people on both sides of me struck up random conversation. Mind you, this was early on a Monday morning and the place was packed with business travelers—these friendly reactions were far from typical. And this was O'Hare, not one of those small airports in some charming southern city where people talk to strangers. At the security check the woman in front of me let me go ahead of her for no obvious reason. All the way to my gate, people were randomly making eye contact and smiling. It was O'Hare in the twilight zone—and it was awesome.

The ultimate freaky experience happened on a trip to New York. As I walked through busy Midtown Manhattan during the morning rush hour, I offered compassion to as many people as I could. Because it was so crowded and people were moving so quickly, I alternated, "May you be well," and "I love you," to each person I could visually pin down. I felt the crowded sidewalks working with me rather than against me. Fast walkers juggling coffee and cell phones made eye contact and smiled. People stepped to the side to allow me and my roller-board suitcase to use the ramp at the curb.

I arrived at the office building I had visited many times before and thought about the receptionist I was about to face. After quite a few meetings with her let me just say she was not the friendliest person I had ever met. My past experiences with her had been short—she rarely looked up from what she was doing and appeared annoyed when I asked her questions. She generally seemed unfriendly and for some reason, that intimidated me.

Feeling the love high from my walk in, I reminded myself that her attitude had nothing to with me. She had no influence over my day. In the elevator ride up to the office, I pictured her and sent her love and compassion. I wished her well, told her she rocked, and told myself that I rocked for vowing to stand strong in my own energy.

What happened when I walked into that office is nothing short of a miracle. Before I had the opportunity to look up toward her desk I heard a loud and friendly, "Good Morning!" This woman who had always been rude and acted like I was bothering her was genuinely nice. She seemed happy to see me. She welcomed me back and without my having to ask, directed me to where my meeting was taking place. She complimented me on my coat and told me the color looked fabulous on me. I'm not kidding.

I would have expected anyone in New York City that morning to pay me a compliment before I would have expected it from her. Unbelievable.

How and Why

What's behind all this?

It could be that since practicing loving-kindness feels so good to me, I radiate a higher energy—a more likeable, more approachable energy. I'm sure that's at least part of it.

It could be that people really can feel when love is directed toward them. They sense it on some level and maybe they associate it with the source.

Either way, I'm not worried about the how or the why. The what is more than enough to keep me playing the mushy love game.

78

Everything You Ever Needed

One of my favorite topics is need. I love it when people tell me they need something they don't have.

Or when they argue that their needs haven't been met.

How could either of those possibly be true? If you truly needed something that you weren't getting—and you are still alive—then you didn't really need it. Right?

Given that you are alive and reading this, it should be pretty obvious that you've always had all of your true needs met. And you always will until you die. If you can live without it, you don't actually need it, right?

What most people call needs are actually wants. Wants are things we'd like to have but we can live without them. So what, you ask? Isn't this simply a semantic argument? Nope. The distinction between needs and wants is very significant.

There's an entirely different energy to, "I need" than there is to, "I want." "I need," sets you up for believing that if you don't get it, you have to suffer. "I want," doesn't as much. And, "I need" puts you in a disempowered place. "I need," usually implies that someone or something else is required for your need to be fulfilled, as in "I need his love," or "I need to be treated in a particular way."

That's a losing formula. If you need it (which means: This is serious! Big danger if I don't get it!) and something outside of yourself is required for your "need" to be fulfilled, well, you are pretty much screwed.

"I want his love," or "I want to be treated a particular way," at least gives you a choice. You can hope they comply but if they don't, you can move on. You can find love or respect elsewhere or abandon your desire altogether. You have choices because there's no need, just a want.

So rest assured that your needs are met. They always have been and as long as you are alive, they always will be. You simply have a want or desire, not a need.

And that's a lot less serious. You can handle a want.

79

Success is So Much
More Likely than Failure

You might not believe me at first but I swear it's the truth–we're infinitely more likely to succeed in life than to fail.

If you think about it, much more goes right in your life than wrong. Even on your worst day ever. I know this doesn't feel true because—in a protective and adaptive way—we're inclined to notice and exaggerate negativity. For example, in a sea of faces we're wired to notice the angry faces faster and more easily than the happy faces. This inclination might seem pessimistic, but it makes sense when your life depends on avoiding angry people who might kill you.

While we're focusing on the relatively few things that go wrong in life, we're totally taking for granted everything that goes right.

- You woke up this morning.
- The sun was up, or on its way up.

- Your limbs and internal organs most likely worked.
- You had access to food.
- You probably had clean, running water with no effort on your part.

This is just a fraction of what effortlessly and automatically went right, within just the first few minutes of your day. Nothing was required of you. You didn't have to do anything or figure anything out; the sun, and your organs, and the water just worked for you.

So isn't it funny that when something goes "wrong," like the train is late or the coffee gets cold or even if something more important happens like getting sick, we perseverate and grossly overemphasize how frequent and how devastating it is?

One thing I like to do to bypass this perceptual error is to imagine I'm someone much less fortunate looking in on my life. I imagine someone who has spent their life in a hospital bed or the guy who lives under the viaduct near my old house in Chicago. Or even someone from another world, like an alien who doesn't understand that you can turn the faucet and get clean water.

I put myself in the place of someone who wouldn't take things like working limbs and running water for granted. How would they perceive the good/bad balance in my life?

When you pay attention and marvel at all the miracles in your life, how do you perceive it?

Part VII

Everyday Enlightenment

"Enlightenment must come little by little - otherwise it would overwhelm".
—Indries Shah

Incredible things begin to happen when you take small steps to become more Enlightened today than you were yesterday.

When you notice your habitual patterns with full awareness and curiosity and you choose new behaviors to replace them. When you stop believing your mental stories and you feel your emotions like a baby. When you speak to yourself the way you would an innocent child and you speak to others with no underlying agenda. When you listen to and honor your intuition.

When you begin to make some of these small shifts, your experience of the everyday is transformed.

You see everything and everyone on earth as more connected than separate—the boundaries between yourself and the rest of the world fade, just a little.

You feel more compassion for people around you. Because you are all on the same team and you have everything you need, the pressure is off. Competition is meaningless and the concepts of scarcity and lack no longer make sense.

You have a new appreciation for Now, without judging it or trying to change it. Now is somehow perfect, exactly as it is.

When you build a little Enlightenment into the everyday, every day is transformed. Are you ready?

80

Gratitude for Being Human

Here's what I'm grateful for right now: being human, and everything that being human entails.

I used to think being human kind of sucked most of the time. Human-ness felt like a big hassle with our habitual patterns that run on auto-pilot, our irrationally fearful thoughts, and our unpredictable emotions. I would fantasize about being super-human; not another species or anything, but one of those people who seemed untouchable and above the petty problems and insecurities of the rest of us. Not just spiritual but über-enlightened. Buddha-like.

Part of me would still love to be led by Spirit so much that it feels other-worldly, but this world—and being human on it—isn't so bad either. My change in thinking came mostly from my clients. This isn't something I normally talk about and it's going to sound cheesy as all get out, but I'm okay with that....

You see, I sort of fall in love with the people who let me into their lives and ask for my opinion. I'm serious about that. It felt weird at first, but I'm starting to really like it. Each time someone is honest about who they are and what they're struggling with, you come face to face with humanity. When they unabashedly share their full-on human-ness, you wonder how you got so lucky.

Every time someone is willing to reveal their imperfections and vulnerabilities…well, it just doesn't get much attractive than that. Why is it so appealing? For one, you get a peak behind the curtain. We all have shame about what's behind our own curtain so when someone lets you peak into their imperfect inner world, you feel more human yourself. You relax a bit about your own imperfections.

There is almost nothing I've ever heard from someone else that I couldn't personally feel or relate to in some way. I know that's true for you, too. We don't all experience things the same way, but the thoughts and feelings that make us human are much the same. Watching someone else bravely feel what you've felt imparts a bond that's indescribable.

So what I'm really grateful for right now is being human—in all its messy vulnerability, emotion, and turmoil. I'm grateful for the friends and clients and honest strangers who have helped me see that imperfections only feel ugly when you hide them. When you are pinching the curtain closed so that no one gets a peak, the thought of being über-enlightened and super-human is very enticing.

But you don't need super powers. All you need is the courage to be human. Trust me, what feels so ugly to you won't look so bad to whomever you are showing it. They might even fall in love with messy, imperfect you.

81

This Is It

Three little words contribute more to my daily happiness than any others: This. Is. It.

This Is It? Yeah, I understand that these words may not flood you with instant bliss. In fact, they may even trigger some despair. This Is It? It doesn't get better than this? Well, it might. Or it might not. But either way, life is right now, today.

I easily get caught up in planning for the future and thinking about the next big thing. I'm always looking for something to generate excitement and keep me anticipating. I'm rarely here, now and because I'm usually somewhere else, I often forget that This Is It. Remembering these words brings me instant joy. It's the little moments in every single day that make up a lifetime.

This Is It.

It is sitting in traffic. What do you do with that time? Do you reflect on a good memory or notice the beauty of the sunrise reflecting off the buildings? Or do you calculate how late you'll be and how that's going to throw off everything else on your schedule? How you really should move to a smaller city because you are wasting your life away in this traffic and besides, the taxes are too high here?

It is what happens at dinner tonight. Do you retell the funny joke you heard, ask the intriguing question that starts a good conversation, or toast your family with your "just" water glasses? Or do you notice that it's "just" grilled chicken again, that it's "just" Tuesday again? Do you use those as excuses to go on autopilot? Are you annoyed that the baby is taking so long to eat her carrots and dropping half of them over the side of her highchair for the dogs? Or do you stick your tongue out at her to make her laugh because her giggles spread to the whole family?

Make no mistake, when it comes to these "It" moments, how you spend them is always your choice. The happy choice is not harder than the less happy choice. We're not talking about booking a cruise around the world or hiking Table Mountain. Sure, those might be big, momentous events that shape your entire life. But a few years' worth of grilled chicken Tuesdays and sitting in morning traffic are nothing to sneeze at, either. They add up.

If you don't believe me, try bettering these everyday occurrences for a while and see what happens. See if your work day doesn't transform, and see if your dinners don't, too. See if your co-workers and your partner and the baby don't all look at you with greater love and admiration. See how much easier it is to make the happier choice when everyone is seeing you that way.

There's nothing to wait for.

You are not getting ready for anything. You are not in preparation. Life is now.

If you are waiting for something before you decide to live full out, be happy, or enjoy the moment, you are gonna miss it.

This is it.

Appendix

If You Want to
Become More Enlightened

If you'd like additional support in becoming more Enlightened, I'd love to help. Here are just a few of the ways I can support you in diving deeper into the Modern Enlightenment concepts and perspectives and applying them to your own life.

Personal Coaching

Work one-on-one with me as your personal coach. Personal coaching consists primarily of regular telephone calls or unlimited, back-and-forth email correspondence—whichever method best fits your life. This is the fastest way to make huge shifts in your thinking and produce big changes in your life. It has changed my life and it can change yours. To learn more about personal coaching visit www.DrAmyJohnson.com/coaching.

Group Coaching and Telecourses

I regularly offer telephone-based classes and coaching groups on special Modern Enlightenment topics. Check www.DrAmyJohnson.com or contact me to see which classes and topics are currently available.

Public Speaking

I would love to speak for your group or event about changing old patterns, thinking in a more Enlightened way, having happy and Enlightened relationships, or any topic that helps people live a better life. I can tailor talks or presentations to your particular group or purpose. Contact me at Amy@DrAmyJohnson.com to plan your event.

Coach Training

I teach people my unique blend of powerful therapy and coaching tools to use in their own life coaching businesses, apply to their own careers, or to simply coach themselves toward more Enlightenement. If you're interested in learning how to coach yourself and others, visit www.DrAmyJohnson.com/life-coach-training-with-amy for more information.

Get My Free eBook and Stay Up-to-Date

For even more support getting out of your own way, you can download my free eBook, *15 Ways You're Blocking Your Own Happiness. And 15 Things to Do Instead* on the homepage at: www.DrAmyJohnson.com. When you sign up there, you'll also receive updates anytime I offer a new coaching opportunity, telecourse, or free product.

About the Author

Dr. Amy Johnson is a psychologist, master certified coach, and public speaker.

She has taught university-level psychology, consulted on several high-profile court cases, spoken to audiences around the country about success and happiness, and sailed around the world.

Amy uses innovative therapy and coaching tools to help clients change old patterns, see the world in a more Enlightened way, and live a life they love. She works with clients worldwide in individual and group coaching programs.

In addition to her work with clients, Amy trains life coaches in her unique methods. She has co-authored a book called *Changes of the Heart: Martha Beck Life Coaches Share Strategies for Facing Life Challenges* and she regularly writes and consults for several online and print publications such as *YourTango* and *Health Magazine*. To find out more about her coaching services, coach training, or to inquire about booking Amy for a speaking event, visit www.DrAmyJohnson.com.